AF614784

Overthinking Mind

*A Counterintuitive Approach to Change Your Life; Unfu*k Yourself, Stop Procrastinating, Eliminate Negativity and Anxiety. Slow Down Your Brain and Be Successful Under All Aspects.*

Yuka Bishop

Table of Contents

Introduction

Thank you for purchasing this book. I hope that you will find it helpful for reducing the likelihood of overthinking, and for reducing the negative impacts that overthinking can have on your mental wellbeing, your career, as well as your life in general. The goal of this book is to help you cultivate a healthy attitude both about yourself and the world and to help eliminate many of the causes of overthinking, such as anxiety and stress. This book serves as an overview of the detailed and expansive literature on such topics, and as such, there is always more to learn and discuss than just what is within these pages. I encourage you to do more research on any of the topics or suggestions that you find interesting. This will not only satisfy your interest but lead to better outcomes for you as an individual. There isn't one technique out there that works for everyone, and so you have to figure out what works best for you, which may or may not be in this book.

This book goes over overthinking and its causes, the way your brain works, procrastination, anxiety, and ways to reduce it, ways of thinking about yourself, and, last but not least, self-actualization.

It's important to clarify exactly what it is we are talking about when we mention "overthinking," and so the first chapter of this book is dedicated to explaining the phenomena, its symptoms, its negative effects, and its causes. Relax and enjoy.

Chapter 1: What Is Overthinking? Why Do We Do It?

You've probably been in this situation before: you're challenged with a project or an assignment, whether it be at work or in school, that should be easy. Something like "develop a strategy for increasing productivity among construction workers." So long as you're calm and get a decent start on it before the deadline, there won't be any problems. But that's not always the case. Sometimes you forget or procrastinate or just blow it off for whatever reason, and by the time you realize that it's due in less than 24 hours, simple things become laborious, puzzling tasks that seem impossible to solve within the time frame. You start to beat yourself up. You reflect on your past mistakes and think, "why do I always do things?" and you worry about your future thinking, "I'm going to mess this up again." That's when you start panicking and produce a product or a result that doesn't live up to your own expectations. This result is a product of *overthinking*.

Overthinking is common in almost every aspect of life, whether it be in a work environment, a social interaction, or even just trying to order food from your local McDonald's. If you're an athlete, you probably experienced it to some degree in games or practice. You get in your own head and start thinking about things that you shouldn't need to. For example, a pitcher in baseball shouldn't *need* to think about how they're swinging their arm down, or how far out they're stepping from the mound, and on a good day, they won't. On off days, however, they overthink, and all of these things they shouldn't need to think about are suddenly brought to the forefront of their mind.

Before we truly begin, it's extremely important to differentiate between problem-solving and overthinking. Not every problem has a simple solution; if you work in an area like health care policy, or nearly any other kind of social work, you know that there is a near-infinite number of variables to account for and what-ifs to consider. Being able to break down complex problems into its parts and then to piece them back together into a cogent solution is a valuable skill to have, and one that takes quite a bit of practice to get good at. This is not what overthinking is. Overthinking takes this sort of thing and goes a step further into an unhealthy boundary. Overthinking involves a near-endless rumination about a problem, a person, and/or about oneself. They worry. Overthinkers can never be satisfied with a solution or an answer. They are hyper-critical, they can't relax or shut their brain off, and they dwell on problems for longer than is necessary. Above all, they do these things without any purpose or goal in mind. They spend all of this time on unhealthy mental activity and only feel and act worse because of it; they gain nothing, and often enough, do nothing to solve problems.

What's striking about most instances of overthinking is that it doesn't usually happen because of the difficulty of some assignment, or because of some convoluted instructions. It starts with the individual. People tend to overthink because of something that *they, themselves*, have done. This is a good thing; if it is something that *you* do, then it is something that *you* can control.

We can break down overthinking into a couple of parts and their causes. This list is by no means exhaustive, but it does cover the most common instances and affects.

Symptoms of Overthinking:

- Panic-like mental state.
- Trying to do too much and overcomplicating the problem.
- Lack of cohesion between thoughts and actions.
- Unclear vision or goal.
- Perceiving the task as being more difficult than it is.
- Perceiving yourself as less skilled than you actually are.
- Lack of enjoyment with the task.
- Not being in the present

If you have one or more of these symptoms, you are probably overthinking, leading to suboptimal performance. The following sections further detail these symptoms.

Panic-Like Mental State

When overthinking, people tend to be mentally chaotic. It is difficult for them to formulate any coherent, full-bodied thought, and for them to stay on any one topic or stream of consciousness for an extended period of time. It might be best described as "scatterbrained." This chaotic mental state is particularly problematic for two reasons: (1) Because you are in mental disarray, it is difficult to catch yourself and to recognize your own mental state. This means that fixing the problem while it can be difficult. (2) Mental disarray feeds on itself, meaning the longer you are in it, the more chaotic it gets, and the harder it is to resolve. Once you do recognize that you are in the panic state, the first thought isn't "how do I stop?" but is instead thoughts of self-doubt, rumination, and greater panic in recognition of one's original panic.

Trying to Do Too Much and Overcomplicating the Problem

Those who overthink tend to do more to create a solution than the problem requires, either adding extra steps or overcomplicating procedures. In day to day experiences, people are asked fairly simple questions that require fairly simple answers. In a normal conversation, you might be asked, "how was your weekend?" to which a standard reply might be, "It was good. I went on a hiking trip out in Franconia. How was yours?" An overthinker might attempt to read between the lines or give an answer that they *think* the other person wants to hear, which ends up either being a lie or not 100 percent truthful. This, in and of itself, creates more problems for the overthinker, which they can then continue to overthink: problems like "what did I tell Bill that

I did last weekend?" or "I don't actually like wine, but because I said I did, I was invited to a wine tasting." If, as an overthinker, you can take a step back to look at a problem, question, or task, and then break it down into its component parts, or simply realize that there is nothing deeper going on here, then you can begin to avoid overthinking.

Lack of Cohesion Between Thoughts and Actions

This is one of the most infuriating symptoms of overthinking. Even though your mind is racing at a million miles an hour, trying to make the correct decision, and switching back and forth between what's right and what's wrong, your body refuses to act or doesn't listen. You could be in a conversation with a cute guy or gal, doing your best at flirting. You're stuck between asking, "could I buy you another drink?" or saying, "I like the shoes that you're wearing." Instead, what comes out of your mouth is, "Could I buy you shoes?" which is not only awkward but also kind of rude.

Unclear Vision or Goal

Overthinking often results in confusion about what you want your desired outcome to be. Chronic overthinkers tend to ruminate rather than take action; they spent more time mentally deliberating than they do actually applying themselves. This symptom is more prevalent when the task is open-ended since the more possibilities there are, the more difficult it is to be satisfied with a choice. People even end up less satisfied with trivial choices, such as the type of pasta sauce you decide to pick at the grocery store. This is known as decision paralysis, when presented with a multitude of options, people tend to freeze up and take more time to decide than if there are fewer options.

Perceiving the Task As Being More Difficult Than It Is

This is the feeling one gets when they think that no matter how long they work on something, or how much effort they put in, they will never meet their goals. It's a feeling of being overwhelmed by some daunting task, where there doesn't seem to be a way to solve the problem at hand. This, in combination with being unable to focus, and being panicked, makes the task seem all the more impossible to complete.

Perceiving Ourselves As Less Skilled Than You Actually Are

People who overthink tend to doubt themselves and what they are capable of. They tend to be overcautious and under ambitious, often afraid to take on more challenging or larger tasks even though they would be more than capable of completing them. The tricky thing is, this sort of self-doubt is a self-fulfilling prophecy; by thinking that you're not good enough, you actually end up performing worse than if you were confident. This worse performance further exacerbates the perception that you aren't good enough.

Lack of Enjoyment With the Task

If you are enjoying the task at hand, you aren't thinking about anything else. You are fully consumed with the present moment, and putting everything into what needs to be done. There aren't any extraneous thoughts. Overthinking is a generally negative experience, which can hinder the enjoyment of anything, whether it be learning to play the piano, enjoying a casual conversation with friends, or writing a journal entry. Those who don't overthink tend to treat the task and the moment as its own reward. They do something because they enjoy it for what it is.

Not Being in the Present

Much like not enjoying the task, overthinkers tend not to enjoy the present moment, or (perhaps a better way of putting it), they never tend to be in the present moment. Overthinkers tend to worry about either the past or the future, either reliving past experiences where they've messed up, or fantasizing about how they're going to screw up again. This is sometimes referred to as a repetition compulsion, in which a person re-lives an event over and over again.

Causes of Overthinking:

- Not understanding the topic at hand.
- Little to no preparation
- Lack of confidence in self.
- Lack of time.
- Poor mental and/or physical state (i.e., lack of sleep, hungry, etc.)
- Reward-oriented thinking, rather than task-oriented thinking.
- Pressure, stress, and fear of failure
- Being unable to accept the past and worrying about the future

The following sections go into more detail about each of these causes.

Not Understanding the Topic At Hand

If you don't understand what it is you are supposed to do, there is no way for you to think clearly. You cannot parse out the unimportant from the important. So everything even tangentially related to the task or topic is of interest, even if they conflict with one another. If I asked you to score a basket in basketball, but you've never played basketball, you should first attempt to understand what doing that entails.

Little to No Preparation

Let's say I asked you, in one week's time, to shoot and score a basket from the free-throw line. You'll get five chances to do so. This task isn't particularly difficult; with a little practice, pretty much everyone could do it with some consistency. If you practice for a half an hour a day, taking a hundred practice shots each day for a week, then you would almost certainly make at least one of the five shots, if not more. With enough preparation, you wouldn't even need to think about how you're shooting the ball, or how to stand or set up; it would be second nature. But if you didn't practice, the chances of you making it would drastically go down. You would be conscious of every little action that you're making, from the feeling of the ball as it rolls off your fingertips, to how awkward you feel trying to synchronize bending and extending your knees and arms.

Lack of Confidence in Self

Even if you practiced for a week straight, shooting the basketball over and over again, it wouldn't mean much if you didn't have confidence in yourself when asked to perform. If you doubt yourself, it also means that you've doubt everything that you've practiced and prepared, and you overthink again: thoughts like "how do I usually shoot this ball?" or "what if I fail?" or "should I change how I shoot?" will lead to worse performance. Lack of confidence makes the task seem more difficult than it is and makes you perceive yourself as less skilled than you actually are. Confident people do not spend a lot of time worrying about themselves, and they trust everything that they have done. They're not thinking about past mistakes, and aren't as anxious about the future. Having faith in oneself is difficult, but it is a skill that anyone can develop.

Lack of Time

If instead of a week of practice, I only gave you a couple of minutes, surely the chances of you making a basket would go down, and you might start to strategize about how best to make a basket rather than just relaxing and trying your best. There is no strategy to overcome a lack of time or a lack of preparation. Good things take time. This is why avoiding procrastination is so important (more on this in chapter 3). Additionally, people tend to feel more pressure from things when they have less time.

Poor Mental and/or Physical State

Being down on yourself, being tired, or any number of negative conditions can cause overthinking. If I'm tired or hungry, I'm adding extraneous thoughts about how tired or hungry I am. My mind isn't thinking about what it should be. Our physical and mental states are interconnected; if I am feeling physically tired, there is a high chance that I will feel mentally tired. Likewise, if I feel mentally tired, then I will likely feel physically tired as well. The good news is that we can use this to our advantage. We can improve our mental health by improving our physical health, and we can improve our physical health by improving our mental health. We need to able to approach health equally, emphasizing both mental and physical health. Being in a poor mental or physical state can also lead to an increase in stress and pressure (more on this later).

Reward-Oriented Thinking Rather Than Task-Oriented Thinking

The term "reward-oriented thinking" refers to thinking about the consequences of the task. Rather than thinking about the task, you are thinking about the grade you might receive, or the money you might get from completion, or the social notoriety. Reward-oriented thinking is like an obsession in that you become purely concerned with the end result, the object, rather than the task itself. This is often harmful; you are not focused on the task, but rather what you will *get* from the task. In doing so, you are also not concerned with doing the task to the best of your abilities, but instead doing the bare minimum in order to receive a reward. It's healthier, and you're less prone to overthink if you learn to enjoy the task itself, rather than the reward. Shooting a basketball, or working on a project should be thought of as its own reward. This applies even in social situations. Say you've met someone at a party, and you like this person, and you want them to like you as well. You are concerned with them becoming your friend, or your partner, or what have you. You end up trying so hard to create a perfect conversation with the person that you come off as insecure or awkward. You'd be better off just enjoying the conversation and the time that you currently have with the person that you like. The technical term for making the activity an end in itself is "autotelic."

Pressure, Stress, and Fear of Failure

This is likely the biggest cause of overthinking, and oftentimes, it encompasses all of the other causes. Simply put, the more worried you are about failing, the more likely you are to overthink. Pressure can manifest in two general ways: external pressure and internal pressure. External pressure comes from other's expectations of you. It could be from your parents, your co-workers, or your boss. Most people want to live up to the expectations of those around them; they think it will make them more loved or respected. Unfortunately, it is so much harder to understand what exactly it is that others expect of us than it is for us to understand our own expectations. It's rare to truly grasp what it is that other people want from us, and in attempting to figure it out, we often exaggerate or fabricate these expectations to an unreasonable degree. We might think our parents want us to get a Ph.D. or be a millionaire when all they really want is for us to be happy and healthy. We get caught up in this idea that if we can't live up to expectations, which means we are a failure, and that we're unworthy of those around us. We stress over every little detail, conforming to what we think is everyone else's standards. Everything must be perfect; nothing can go wrong; we must conceive of every possible scenario in order to prepare. We can never *stop* thinking. In reality, these expectations don't actually exist.

Internal pressure is the other kind of pressure. This sort of pressure is endogenous, coming from within. It's about who you expect to be as a human being, and what you want to do in order to reach your goals. This pressure is controllable, though exercising control is not always easy. As with everything in life, we are regulating internal pressure is a balancing act. If we are experiencing too much pressure, then we become perfectionists. Nothing can ever be done right, and we must redo everything. We can never be satisfied with who we are or the work we have done. We are constantly overthinking what it is we need to do to be satisfied, never realizing the problem lies in our own expectations. On the other hand, too little pressure means we have no motivation to change, and no call to action.

It's important to note that a little bit of pressure, fear, and/or stress is still a good thing. We do not want to eliminate *all* of it, just most of it, in order to lead a healthier lifestyle. In fact, eliminating all of it is not only unhealthy but impossible. Stress moves people to action; it's what gets people out of their houses and into the street to protest and make a change. We need stress and pressure, but it should not control what you do or who you are.

Negative effects of overthinking:

- Sub-optimal workflow
- Creating additional problems
- Anxiety
- Self-consciousness
- Depression

The last part of this chapter focuses on the negative effects of overthinking, of which there are many.

Sub-Optimal Workflow

The scatterbrained nature of overthinking makes streamlining your workflow rather difficult. Good workflow demands that everything be in its right place so that you barely need to think about what to do next or what the correct course of action is. In cooking, there is a concept called mise-en-place, which translates into "set in place" in English. It refers to having everything prepared and ready to go before you actually begin cooking. Things are cut how they need to be; they're measured out and separated into different bowls, the oven is preheated, you have a pot of water boiling, you have salt on hand, etc. Doing this work beforehand makes the actual process of cooking much easier. It becomes more about having the correct timing and temperature rather than it being a mad dash to prepare everything before the custard overcooks. You don't need to multitask as much, and you don't need to switch between actively preparing, waiting, timing, and all of the other things involved in making a good meal. In the same way, we want to make sure that we have our mise en place for our workflow.

And not only a physical mise-en-place but a mental mise-en-place is important. We need to have the right state of mind and the right way of thinking about how to perform our actions in order to have an optimal workflow. We need to make the necessary preparations beforehand, both physically and mentally, in order to stop overthinking, and in order to prevent it from beginning in the first place. However, it is a bit of a catch-22. Mise-en-place may help you stop overthinking, but if you *already* overthink, then it can be difficult to coordinate your mise-en-place.

Creating Additional Problems (That May or May Not Exist)

Overthinkers are bad at simplifying problems. Generally speaking, they tend to consider and plan for possibilities that will never occur, or at the very least, are unlikely to occur in any realistic way. In effect, they add on to problems rather than simplify them. The what-ifs pile on and solutions to the original problem become more difficult because they have to account for more and more things, even if the original problem didn't ask for it. In doing so, they are also wasting their time and energy, which creates additional problems as well. They can overthink these problems as well.

Anxiety

Overthinkers are anxious. Anxiety can arise for a variety of reasons, but those reasons are often exaggerated because of overthinking. Understanding anxiety is crucial to understanding overthinking since anxiety is both a product and a cause of overthinking. The entirety of chapter 4 is dedicated to anxiety and its reduction.

Self-Consciousness

Overthinkers don't just overthink about external events or problems; they also overthink when it comes to themselves. They tend to be overly critical of their flaws and undervalue their good characteristics. They also tend to overthink the effect that they have on other people while putting their own interests on the backburner. They don't prioritize themselves, because there are so many other things on their mind. If you overthink, there is a high chance that you blame yourself for everything that goes wrong, even if the things that do go wrong are out of your control.

Depression

Overthinkers tend to be prone to depression or depression-like thoughts. Because they consider so many possibilities, they feel as though there is nothing they can do to live up to their own or external possibilities possibly. No matter how much they do, it will never be enough. Much like anxiety, depression, and depressive thoughts are both a product and a cause of overthinking.

If you or someone you know has depression, suicidal thoughts, or thoughts of hurting themselves or others, please seek help from a certified professional, particularly if you have a family history of depression. Contact a trained therapist in your area or speak to your doctor if possible. There are also a number of free resources available to you. If you live in the United States, you can reach the suicide hotline for free by calling 1-800-273-8255. Do not hesitate to use the resources available to you. It does not make you weak, or unworthy of love, or any of the other ridiculous stigmas attached to seeking treatment for mental health. Know that there are people who are out there who love you, support you, and want to see you get better.

If you are an overthinker, it's likely that you see these negative effects in your own life, and are trying to do something about it without eliminating the root cause of it. You need to do something about how you see yourself, how you feel about yourself, and how you think about yourself. You need to develop healthy routines and habits which can get you out of a slump. You need to cultivate discipline and have a confident, unflinching attitude towards success—the rest of this book details more specific ways of going about doing all of this.

Chapter 2: Understanding You and Your Brain

Let's begin with some basic brain anatomy. We could easily spend an entire chapter on just this subject, but for now, we will highlight some of the more important areas when it comes to understanding behavior and behavioral processes. This part of the chapter is a very brief overview of a very complicated and still developing field of psychology, biology, and neuroscience, and as such, some of these concepts may be oversimplified. There are a number of great resources available online with a quick google search if you wish to have a more in-depth understanding of the topic.

The different parts of the brain are responsible for different things. One of the most important brain areas for humans is the prefrontal cortex, which is situated at the very front of the brain. This part of the brain is responsible for conscious, effortful thought, and for holding and transforming information which is stored in short-term and working memory. When you are told to remember a phone number, you probably are repeating the number over and over in your head. This is your prefrontal cortex at work. It is also used in other high-level cognitive processes such as arithmetic and long term planning. The prefrontal cortex is the thing that helps you work towards your goals, and so it is vitally important to long term success. It is necessary for learning. Unfortunately, it is also the part of the brain that is overactive when overthinking.

Another important part, or rather, area of the brain, is the deep structures. This area of the brain is responsible for most of the things we do without consciously thinking, controlling behaviors, and tasks such as eating, sleeping, emotion, hormonal production, homeostasis, and sexual response. The three parts of the brain that I'd really like to highlight here are part of the limbic system, which is responsible for emotions, learning, and memory. These three things drive almost all behavior, and so it's useful to know just exactly what is going on up there. Within the limbic system, the hypothalamus is the control center. Its job is to regulate all the things mentioned previously (i.e., eating, sleeping, emotion). The amygdala is another part of the limbic system and is one of the oldest and most primal parts of the brain. It handles emotional reactions; in particular, it handles anger and fears the most. Since the dawn of man, fear has played the biggest role in making sure we survive as a species; without it, we wouldn't intuitively know that trying to fight a tiger is a bad idea. The only other thing that can be just as powerful is sexual impulse, which at times, can overcome the threat of fear. Lastly, there is the hippocampus, which is the center for long term memory. Memory is an obviously important function for human beings and one of the things which makes us who we are as individuals.

Something is usually going wrong within these areas of the brain when it comes to overthinking. A hypothalamus that is out of whack will affect all of our naturally occurring processes, making crucial bodily behaviors like sleep difficult to perform consistently. An overly sensitive amygdala will create more fear or anxiety than is appropriate given the situation, making us feel worse than we should, and driving erratic behavior in order to quell the stress response. The hippocampus needs to be kept in check so that we are not endlessly ruminating on our past experiences.

The actions controlled by the cerebellum are somewhat in-between these sorts of extremes when it comes to voluntary versus involuntary behavior. The cerebellum is primarily involved in motor functions, including balance, posture, voluntary movement, and motor function and learning, although its responsibilities do extend out into the cognitive domain. In particular, the cerebellum helps us learn motor skills through feedback mechanisms wherein it coordinates our movements with our desired outcomes in the world (usually as per the prefrontal cortex dictates), working on a sort of trial and error basis to see what actions are working and what actions aren't. A good example of this is learning to throw a pitch in baseball. If you throw a good strike, that registers as a good movement, which raises the likelihood of being able to repeat this action, and is strengthened through even more practice. On the other hand, a wild pitch or a ball will not register as a good pitch, and so we will try to avoid the sort of movement pattern that produced this poor result. This mechanism is precisely why practice and repetition are so important to improve in all domains, both cognitive and physical. It is also why mental visualization and repetition allows us to improve our physical actions, even if we are not physically practicing.

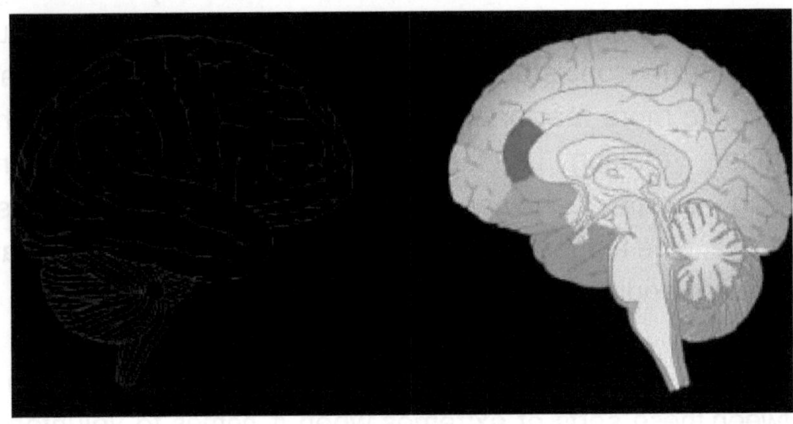

All of these areas are deeply interconnected, working together to form the thing that we call consciousness. But, there is a lot going on under the hood as well, things that were not even aware of and cannot possibly be aware of. Our brain likes to fill in the gaps and make assumptions about what is happening. As you will see, the assumptions are hit-or-miss. For the most part, and in everyday circumstances, our brain can make fairly accurate automatic judgments about things (i.e., how to open a door, how to read). However, it also has a tendency to try to protect our well-being and self-esteem, which is a double-edged sword, as it makes us feel good, but can lead to distorted views of the self. Having an accurate depiction of who you are and what goes on in terms of psychological processes can be upsetting. The reason that most people tend to have a depiction of themselves that is better than what is reality is that your brain does it's best, in most instances, to make you feel good about yourself; we call this your "psychological immune system," and it's critical to have a healthy psychological immune system in order to cultivate resilience and bounce back from failure. However, it is also true that people with depression tend to have a more accurate depiction of their abilities than people without depression, which is a depressing fact in and of itself. A lot of this book is about walking the fine line between a negative, morbid reality and having a healthy idea of who you are. You want to know that you have room to grow and change while being able to recognize both your current limitations and your current accomplishments.

If you are at your wits end in terms of anxiety, stress, or overthinking, or if you are having difficulties sleeping, eating, or performing other normal bodily functions, so much so that not even medication in combination with therapy helps, it may be helpful to see a neurologist. This may sound extreme and scary to some (or most) people, but I can assure you that the doctor is not going to do or recommend anything drastic. The most they will do is offer to schedule either a CT Scan or an fMRI to see if there is something going on up in the brain. These procedures are harmless, and even if they had the potential to be dangerous, they are usually not necessary.

We'd like to think that we are the ones who are in control of our brains, but the fact is, most of our brain processes are automatic. We cannot exercise any *direct* control over how our brain responds to various situations or stimuli. If you see a bear running towards you, you have a fight-or-flight reaction. If your mother hugs you, your brain releases oxytocin. Over thousands of years, our brain has evolved to have the appropriate responses to these stimuli in order to facilitate our survival. If we didn't want to run away from a bear, we would die. Likewise, having that warm, fuzzy feeling from hugging a family member teaches us to create tight-knit groups that are more likely to survive than any one individual is. The thing is, there is almost no way to escape from the evolutionary constraints placed on our brain, unless through heavy drugs or brain surgery. It's extremely difficult to convince our brains that a predator coming to kill us isn't scary, or that a warm hug doesn't feel good. The limbic system holds particularly strong sway over our immediate reactions to external stimuli.

Moreover, these automatic processes are incredibly efficient. They are so quick that they happen even without our conscious awareness of it. I don't need to think about being scared by the bear, or feeling loved by my mother, I just am. It's as natural as breathing and digesting. Imagine if we *did* need to contemplate these sorts of things, and what a strange experience it would be. I don't want to and shouldn't need to think about if I'm feeling scared or loved. It would be a waste of my time and energy to consciously deliberate about these things. We need to accept that it is often a good thing that certain reactions are inherently outside of our control. That being said, there are a number of things that we can't automatically deal with, and there are cases where our automatic processes create wrong answers. Automatic processes often use mental shortcuts (i.e., heuristics) in order to simplify problems based on previously recognized patterns. It's why we can immediately know that two plus two equals four, but it's also why we are susceptible to the sunk-cost fallacy. We make snap judgments on almost anything; some people may call it a "gut reaction."

One of the best things about the human brain is that it is well equipped to handle novel situations. We're lucky enough to have the sort of consciousness which allows for things like an inner monologue and deliberative thought. We can plan, create, organize, and turn our thoughts into action with relative ease. We can experiment, try out solutions, redo, and theorize. We can write, speak, argue, and converse with both others and ourselves in order to find the best solution to whatever the problem at hand is. Most of our education is built around developing and refining our ability to think deeply. All of this is certainly a blessing, but with that being said, *thinking is so much more difficult than not thinking (at least when it comes to performance measurements).*

We can separate our brain processes into two different systems, unoriginally named System 1 and System 2. Psychologist Daniel Kahneman expressed the differences between these two systems in his book Thinking, Fast and Slow. System 1 processes are the automatic processes that are not in conscious awareness. These processes are heavily involved in the execution of actions. When we open a door, we don't think about how our hand is grasping the doorknob, or how to twist and pull it open. The areas of the brain associated with these behaviors include the limbic system, the basal ganglia (which is responsible for finer, smaller movements), and the hippocampus. On the other hand, System 2 processes are the slow, deliberate, and effortful processes involved in goal-oriented tasks, often necessary for solving novel or difficult problems. We might think of

System 2 as the command center; it tells us that we should leave the room. The prefrontal cortex is the most important area of the brain for System 1 processes, although the cerebellum helps as well. These processes work together, with System 2 handling the overarching decisions and planning, and System 1 handling the minutia.

Our brain is super lazy. It naturally wants to conserve energy. It will put off as much as it possibly can onto unconscious, automatic processes. When it comes to overthinking, this is a good thing. *Overthinking occurs when thoughts and actions that should be automatic become slow and deliberate.* In other words, ordinary System 1 processes turn into System 2 processes. Something that should be automatic, such as tying your shoes, or having a casual conversation with a partner, becomes something that you need to think about. However, we also want to avoid having the opposite problem: underthinking. In this case, System 2 processes turn into System 1 processes. We might think of this issue as going on auto-pilot, like when you get into your car and drive to work even though it's your day off. In short, we want to optimize our brain's performance by delegating the appropriate tasks to System 1 processes or System 2 processes.

If we return to sports, we can see a concrete example of this optimal processing. A professional athlete who has practiced enough does not need to think about the way in which his body moves: he doesn't need to think about how to run, or how to swing a bat, or throw a ball, or field a grounder, etc. These are all system 1 processes that have been ingrained in him through constant repetition and practice. However, this isn't all there is to sports, and it is just as much a mental game as a physical game. Every individual match is different, each with unique and novel instances. Some problems cannot be answered solely through System 1 processes. If a runner decides to steal, what should I do? What pitch should I throw next? Should I walk the batter and load the bases, or pitch to contact, or try to strike him out? These sorts of questions are the responsibility of System 2 processes. Yet these two systems are not entirely separate. Optimal performance requires both of them. Without System 2, the athlete will not accurately make or decide on the correct decision, and without System 1, the athlete will not be able to execute the action. System 1 and System 2 are in harmony.

Now that we've discussed two of the ways in which your brain works, you might be wondering, "well, that's great, but how do I affect these processes? How can I hijack my own brain in order to optimize performance and avoid overthinking (or underthinking)?" As mentioned previously, we can't really change the way our brain works *directly*. We can't simply tell our brain to choose what to process automatically, and what to process deliberately. We can, however, indirectly affect the way in which our brain works through our environment, and through our habits.

Our environment plays a key role in determining how our brain processes and response to information. One simple example of this is distractions: when you're trying to concentrate on a project, having a person who is trying to talk to you can be incredibly frustrating. You don't stay on task, you keep having to change your attention, and overall, your workflow is incredibly inefficient. This can lead to some of the causes of overthinking mentioned in chapter one: not having enough time, poor mental state, and reward-oriented thinking. The more that our mind wanders, the more likely we are to focus on irrelevant and harmful things; we may ruminate about the past, or worry about the future, or over-analyze ourselves and our behavior.

The simplest solution is to control your environment. If you're working on a project at home, try to find a nice, quiet place. Don't turn on the tv, don't turn on your phone, make a warm cup of tea and relax before getting into your workflow. Take some deep breaths and meditate. Tell yourself that you only need to get started, that you'll only work for five minutes. By the time you think five minutes is up, you'll probably have more done than you thought possible, and you're ready to do more. Preventing overthinking is, as previously mentioned, a balancing act. If you have nothing to focus on, then your mind is free to wander, leading to overthinking and rumination. If you have too much to focus on, then your mind goes from task to task, to task, and is never productive. When there is too much to do, it is easy to get overwhelmed. This creates self-doubt, increases the perception of difficulty, produces stress and pressure, and increases worry.

Of course, sometimes it's difficult to control the environment completely. If you're in a crowded bar, there's no doubt that you will be faced with plenty of distractions and interruptions, which might make it difficult to stop yourself from overthinking. Let's say your goal is just to have a good night out, and talk to some strangers, and maybe make some friends. You don't want to be thinking about how to *make friends best*. That, in itself, takes away from the focus on the present moment and makes it harder to enjoy the time that you have out. Distractions may include the fact that the DJ is playing the music far too loud, meaning you have to yell in order to be heard. There may be some obnoxious drunk couple making a scene at the table behind you. Or maybe the bar smells like cigarettes, and you can't seem to ignore it. Any number of these things can cause you to overthink: "why can I never have a good time when I go out?", or "I can't wait to go home and get some sleep" or, "I wish I could change the situation I'm in" are all common thoughts to have when overthinking in social scenarios. These thoughts cause you to act differently than if you were relaxed and comfortable. You end up forcing things to happen rather than just acting naturally. Maybe you laugh at a joke even if it's not that funny, or maybe you end up being overly talkative in hopes that people will notice you. Maybe, then, because none of these things have worked, you end up brooding in the bathroom for twenty minutes, wishing you could just disappear. Maybe you don't go out again for months at a time because you're worried about repeating the same night.

When in an uncontrollable environment, the best thing to do is fall back on a routine. This routine can be mental or physical, whichever best helps you to calm down and to remind yourself why you're doing something in the first place. One common thing that people do is to bring their focus back to one thing, usually some sensation in the present moment. It could be the beer that you're sipping on, the feeling of the bar stool that you're sitting on, or even just how hot or cold it is in the room. Sensations are a powerful tool; they serve as reminders of the present moment. They tell us who and what we are. They tell us that what we are experiencing is normal and that we've done this before and ended up ok. A negative example of this technique is pain. If you've ever broken a bone or been in any other sort of serious pain, you'll notice how difficult it is to focus on anything else besides that pain. I've read stories of Navy Seals purposefully injuring themselves in order to bring back their focus to whatever it is they need to do. Naturally, however, we don't want to injure ourselves just to avoid overthinking. The previously mentioned solutions are viable alternatives.

Once you've picked out a sensation to focus on, sit on it for a while. The goal here is to have that sensation be the only thing on your mind. By focusing so heavily on one thing, you can empty your mind of all of the other thoughts in your head, and return yourself to the present. As you might have guessed, this isn't always as easy as it sounds. After all, it requires that you *remember* to do these things while in an overthinking state, which is difficult. Like any other skill, it takes practice. There are other routines that you can try, as well—more on this in chapter 4.

The vital components of affecting your brain processes are practice and repetition. Most things, other than eating, breathing, sleeping, start out as System 1 processes. Think back to learning to tie your shoes as a little kid. You didn't automatically or subconsciously know how to do it. You likely had to learn to do it from a parent, teacher, or older sibling. When they taught you, they likely also could not just show you the maneuvers. They probably gave you step by step verbal instructions, complete with helpful mnemonics, like "making bunny ears" or "doing a loopty-loop." Additionally, you likely did not successfully tie your shoes the first time you attempted to do so. It probably took you dozens of tries, with your teacher showing you how to do it dozens of times. All of this was for just one successful attempt. You still had to consciously think about the moves you were doing, what it should look like, how your fingers should be positioned, etc. It's only after a countless repetition that tying your shoes became automatic, and something that you didn't have to think about.

Most skills are like this. Driving a car, typing on a keyboard, and even reading all took a conscious effort to do at first. Remember when you had to sound out words even to come close to pronouncing them correctly? Now, you read words even if you don't want to. I have a challenge for you. Keep looking at this book, but don't read it. Try not to process what this sentence is saying. I can almost guarantee that this is impossible for you. If you see words, you automatically read them, for better or for worse. And what's shocking about this is, not only do you read automatically, you are *really good* at reading automatically. Sure, if a word is uncommon, you may have trouble deciphering it at first, but for the most part, and especially for common words or phrases, the error rate in parsing the words is fairly low. It's not like reading is this simple thing, either. It's an incredibly complex system of communicating ideas and meaning. You have to know what the words are, what they mean, how they can be put together, and the whole of the sentence means something that is greater than the sum of its component parts. Native language speakers will intuitively know when something sounds wrong. Figuring out the meaning of language is something that even high-level computers have trouble doing, and yet with enough practice, your brain does it with ease.

There are many ways to practice, with some being more effective than others. This book will cover a few of them. Keep in mind that some techniques will help you more than others, depending on the type of person that you are. Some people benefit from more direct, outwardly facing techniques, and some people benefit from inward-facing, harder to grasp ways of looking at a skill or idea.

Let's begin with some basics. These ideas are applicable to any form of practice, no matter how complicated or basic it may be, You should especially follow these tips when you are just beginning to learn a skill. If you are learning how to do something, there is a critical period in the beginning. People learn most effectively when they are younger, and can absorb more information when just beginning to learn something. The two biggest examples of this are in language and soccer. Let us look at bilingual children for a second. If you are in the United States and are naturalized as a citizen, chances are that you only learned to speak one language, that being English. Obviously, that is ok and even necessary. If you only need to learn one language to thrive in the great USA, then why should you even bother to learn another? The United States could learn from the difference in cultures, and god forbid, could use that difference to improve its own infrastructure. Alas, that isn't always the case. Many sons and daughters are only exposed to just one language. In fact, if we look at most modern American families, they are not bilingual; they only speak English. The fact that they do this isn't really any fault of their own; it is just a result of the environment that they grew up in. And that is how it is with everyone. No matter who you are, you have the opportunity to learn a different language. If you were born on the border of France and Germany, chances are, you know, French, German, and English (since that is the "communicative" languagebetween the two).

When you begin to learn a skill or idea, it is easier the younger than you are. Let's look at some examples. One of the best soccer players in the world, Lionel Messi, is an example of what it takes to become a paragon of soccer and skill throughout the world. Messi was born in 1987, in Argentina, to a relatively low-income family. However, he began to play soccer when he was four years old, and not against his peers, but against people who were much older than he was. In order to thrive in this competitive environment, he needed to adapt quickly. When you are young, your brain is much more plastic, and you can easily absorb information. While the majority of the people reading this are probably over the age of 20, there is still an important lesson we can take away from this; the earlier you start to practice, the easier it becomes in the future.

There are a couple of basics to practice that everyone can learn from. The first is to start slowly. There isn't a skill there that can be learned from being thrust into a real-life, high-pressure situation. Pressure is only good when you are proficient in skill since pressure can bring out the best of your abilities and improve focus if honed enough. But when you're first starting out, try to be as comfortable as possible.

The other thing to remember is to take breaks. You don't want to burn yourself out doing the same thing over and over. It's important to stay motivated and disciplined if you want to see quicker and better results. Not stopping, while in some cases admirable, will burn you out. Studies have shown that 30 to 45 minutes of intense, focused practice, followed by 5 to 10 minutes of time off, is the most efficient way to practice. It is also the most sustainable way of practicing since it gives you a reasonable time to recover. Generally speaking, you get diminishing returns when it comes to practice, with you improving less the longer that the practice session goes on. This is because people get tired or lose focus, and so they can't properly execute what they need to in order to improve. If you're going to take anything about practice, remember this: practice does not make perfect. Perfect practice makes perfect. You need to go slow and take time to do things properly. There is no short-cut here, no magical thing that will make you better overnight (although you do need to sleep in order to learn and improve). You just have to put in as many close to perfect repetitions as you can.

Lastly, when it comes to practice, remember that it is normal to plateau and to see diminishing returns over an extended period of time. Know that you will not see the same improvement in the eighth month of training that you had in the first month of training. If you are really stuck, two things may help: (1) Switch up your training regimen. Try out new things, experiment, see what works for you. (2) Take a longer break. Take a week off from practice. A lot of practice is just mental. Give your brain some time to reset. And speaking of the brain, it's important to have the right attitude when it comes to practice. It is important to act like a beginner as much as possible. Don't have any preconceptions about your skills, and don't close your mind to the possibility that what you have been doing isn't optimal; you can always improve *how* you improve. Just because you can do something well does not mean you cannot improve further, or that you should stop making changes to it. In Japanese, there is a term called "shoshin," which translates to "beginner's mind." If you are interested in a more detailed analysis of the concept, I recommend that you check out the book *Zen Mind, Beginner's Mind* by Zen monk Shunryu Suzuki. There are many ways to foster shoshin. One way is to try to have an accurate view of just how good you are at something, or how much you know. You do not want to have the idea that you are a big fish just because you are swimming in a tiny pond, especially if you haven't seen the ocean. Understand that it is a big world out there. Try to teach someone what you have learned and see if when you do so, they can follow it easily, or maybe you'll have a feeling that you have left out something. It's ok to have to relearn things yourself. Know that confirmation bias exists (which we will talk about very soon). Be aware that you still have room to grow and improve.

The last portion of this chapter will be about how your brain makes decisions. We've already talked about System 1 and System 2 processes, and these concepts still apply to what I'm about to say. I'm going to talk about the role that emotions play in determining decisions, and how to address concerns that this may cause.

Here is an immutable psychological fact: people aren't really affected by logic, at least when it comes to things like changing their minds, evaluating their stances, or making the correct decision. We are decidedly the sorts of creatures that rely on their gut and their intuition. Most people have this sort of idea about how they think decisions are made. First, they look at the facts. Then they use the facts to come to a reasoned conclusion as to what should be the case or what is correct. If you think about a judge presiding over a trial, you would hope that this is how decisions are made, since it seems the fairest. Unfortunately, this isn't actually what happens according to modern psychology. Decision making and judgments actually occur in the reverse order. People form the conclusion that they want or would like to see, usually something that is favorable towards them, then they pick and choose the facts that best support this judgment. This is a form of confirmation bias, in which people only seek or notice facts that support what they already believe. This is extremely common in politically charged or controversial topics where people are anchored in their ways. Let's look at the topic of gun ownership rights as an example. The people who tend to support gun ownership will usually own guns themselves. They tend to be right-leaning on the political spectrum and live in more rural areas. Those who oppose allowing gun ownership usually do not own guns themselves. They are more left-leaning on the political spectrum and tend to live in more metropolitan areas. Let me ask you a question: do you think that any of these people on either side of the political spectrum came to their original conclusion on whether people should be allowed to own guns or not did so through a careful, studied, or factual analysis of the pros and cons of gun ownership? If there is anyone who did so, they are the exception, not the rule. They probably decided whether to support gun ownership or not, not based on facts, but based on their exposure to guns, the attitude of the people around them, their upbringing, their political affiliation, etc. All these things play a larger role in forming their judgments, decisions, and dispositions than facts or logic ever could. It is only after they have already made a decision that they begin to pick out the facts that support it, and that usually only occurs when they have to defend their beliefs from others who disagree with them. There's a saying that I like, which states that you don't actually know what you think until you have to defend it.

As I said before, most decisions and judgments are made like this, even important ones. Even greater difficulties can arise because most people either don't realize what is driving their decisions or are misguided in mistaking their subjective feelings and emotions for subjective facts and logic. The latter is far more dangerous for two reasons: (1) it's much harder to convince the person who does this that they are, in fact, driven by emotions, and (2) it is typically a symptom of people who know more about the topic (i.e., the more you know, the less you think your own feelings influence you).

This rule isn't ironclad. There are people and instances where people are able to draw conclusions from well-reasoned arguments or facts, although it is rare. Typically, there is more objectivity in things like science, and less in things like politics.

So we want to avoid the trap of mistaking our feelings for facts, and we want to realize when our emotions are driving us. Doing so should help us to make better, more informed decisions leading to better outcomes. We can't prevent our emotions from doing a lot of the heavy lifting in our thinking, nor can we really influence factors like how our parents raised us, or genetics, or where we grew up. That's all a matter of luck. But, what we can do is ask questions about all of these things. When you are trying to form a judgment on something, look at all of the possible reasons for why you think that. This includes looking at our histories and knowing how we are feeling. When we do so, we can understand how we came to make a decision, and we can make a decision about that decision. We can ask, is this decision reasonable, or am I just making it based on our impulse?

Chapter 3: Procrastination

Procrastination is a common problem for most people. It can occur for any number of reasons, with the most common one being a lack of motivation, which in itself can be caused by a wide range of things. Procrastination is problematic in a similar way to anxiety and depression; once you begin procrastinating, it is difficult to stop doing so because of the nature of what procrastination is, namely, delaying what you *should* be doing in favor of doing something else.

The best way to avoid procrastination is to be disciplined in your actions. In other words, you should be so accustomed to your routine or habits that *not* doing your daily routine should lead to discomfort. Some people may already be familiar with the sensation; perhaps you are accustomed to going to bed after a shower or brushing your teeth. If you don't do these things, you may be unable to fall asleep. The idea is to make success and your workflow part of your daily habit. Success doesn't need to be objectively measured; it simply needs to be a measure of some sort of progress. Success is generally subjective; if you feel you are making progress, you probably are. Let's say you make it a goal of writing 2000 words every single day. At the present moment, you are writing less than 200 words a day. After a week or so of setting this goal, you end up writing 1000 words a day. Does this mean that you are a failure for not meeting your aspirational goal? Absolutely not! You've made significant progress, even if you haven't exactly met what you set out to do. There's a reason why people tell you to aim high: "Shoot for the moon. Even if you fail, you'll end up among the stars." You don't need to set a personal record every single day. Technically speaking, you don't even need to improve every single day statistically.

One of the best analogies to give comes from weightlifting. If you are interested in weightlifting, generally, that means that you are interested in getting stronger. If you currently squat 200 pounds, you might want to set a goal of squatting 300 pounds. What do you think is the best way of getting to your goal? One approach that people *might* think works is progressively maxing out each day. You start out at 200 pounds, then the next session you move up to 205 pounds, then 210, then 215, 220, 225, etc. While this may seem reasonable at first, you'll find that doing this sort of training program burns people out extremely quickly. You basically give your body no time to rest, no time to adapt to the current stimuli, and you end up only being able to handle the program for a couple of days. It is unhealthy to expect that you'll set new records everytime you attempt them.

A better way of approaching improvement is gradual adaptation. If the maximum weight that you can squat is 200 pounds, you wouldn't just want to try to increase the weight each time you squat. You're not actually getting stronger. Instead, what you'll want to do is lower the weight a little bit, let's say down to 175 pounds. You squat 175 pounds for five reps at a time, for five sets, for maybe a week. After that amount of time, you adapt to the weight, with it getting easier as you go. The next week, you repeat the same pattern at 180 pounds, then 185 pounds, then 195 pounds, etc. A month or two later, you test how much you can squat again, never having gone beyond squatting more than 200 pounds. With your training, however, you end up squatting 225 pounds.

We can take two very important lessons from weightlifting: (1) When trying to improve, you don't need to expend maximum effort every time you train in order to see gains. (2) Consistent repetition is far more beneficial than sporadic sessions.

Lesson (1) tells us to correct our misconceptions about improvement. Improvement is not the sort of thing that happens overnight. We cannot correct all of our mistakes or bad habits through brute force. The only way to truly improve is to take a step back to correct the basics; to improve the "form," so to speak. Sure, we might be able to grind out a few extra pounds on the squat by sacrificing the structural integrity of our back and knees, but at what cost? Some skewed sense of pride or dignity? Who actually cares if you can squat 205 pounds instead of 200 pounds, especially if you like you might collapse during the former repetition? You don't actually gain anything from it; you don't improve, you don't grow any stronger. You just boost your own ego and vanity, which can never be healthy. There is a massive difference between confidence in yourself and having an ego. It's far better to leave the ego at the door, take a step back, and actually improve. In doing so, and in having the right mindset, you won't get burned out. Just imagine how stressful it is to have the expectation of creating a new personal record every time you attempt something; where if you don't *constantly* and *instantly* improve at every new instance, it's deemed a failure. That's exhausting, not only on a physical level but on a mental level. Sustaining a positive attitude about oneself and about one's improvement with this sort of expectation is just not possible. The fact is, sometimes you'll have good days, and you'll have bad days. Sometimes you'll be well-rested, full of energy, and in a good mood. On these days, you're more likely to show vast improvement, particularly if the previous day was one where you had poor sleep or poor mental health. This is where the second lesson comes in.

Lesson (2) tells us that the most important thing for any sort of improvement is consistency. You'll hear successful people say things like "no days off" or "keep on the grind," and that's for a good reason. Successful people don't just look for success in a day's time. They look for improvement across months, years, or even decades. Chess masters are not born as such; most of them only improve a couple of ranks per *year* (with some exception). It is never healthy to measure yourself by your day to day performance. Just because you've squatted 225 pounds one day does not mean you will be able to do so the next day. Maybe you will only get 210 pounds due to some other variable. But in a month's time, the average amount you can squat, with constant training, *will go up*. In two months, it will go up again, as it will in three, four, or twelve. However, we must be careful not to overdo it. Giving your body and mind the opportunity to rest and recover is critical to any sort of improvement. Recovery can be considered both a part of training and a part of discipline; you are disciplined enough to take a break, and then return to your normal routine.

Another thing to keep in mind with improvement is that you will seem markedly more improved when you first start to improve than later on down the line. In weightlifting, this is known as “newbie gains” because new weightlifters will be able to improve far more quickly than veterans of the sport. It’s not uncommon for new weightlifters to increase their weight by 50 pounds in a specific exercise within a month. For a veteran weightlifter, however, increasing by 50 pounds may take years if it is even possible at all. People are fairly good at learning new things, and we can generally become proficient with some time dedicated to whatever it is we want to improve in. Just know that you do not improve linearly. In mathematical terms, most people improve logarithmically, with the most notable improvements coming at the beginning of one’s journey.

We want to apply these lessons to our daily habits. We can’t expect ourselves to be maximally productive every single day, but we can set short term goals and long term goals for ourselves. However, some goals are better than others. Here are some examples of *not so good* goals.

- Do more, every day, than the day I have previously.
- Write a novel.
- Get in shape.

- Run a marathon.

At first glance, these all seem like pretty good long term goals to have, and they would be if they had some plan around them. None of these goals have a plan built around them, which makes them seem like daunting tasks, and can make measuring progress towards them difficult. Here are some examples of better goals.

- Do *something* every day
- Write 500 words a day.
- Go to the gym five times a week.
- Eat at least one serving of vegetables a day.
- Run 10 miles over the course of a week.

The goals aren't as daunting, and they aren't so far off that you can't measure your progress or if you've met these goals. We want our success to be measurable; otherwise, it is easy to get discouraged by not meeting your own goals. It's also easy to get started on these goals. If you want to write 500 words a day, you can probably finish a 100 words by the time you finish your morning coffee, and once you're in the midst of writing 100 words, the next 200 or 300 will come more easily. The same sort of thought can be applied to other goals. You can set a reminder for yourself to go to the gym after work. You'll notice that this goal doesn't say anything about how hard you have to work at the gym, only that you should go. Once you're at the gym, *you* decide what you'll do, how difficult it will be, how long you will stay, etc. If you want to eat at least one serving of vegetables a day, *buy* vegetables that you enjoy eating. When you're at the grocery store, make it a point of using the money you would normally spend on chips for broccoli instead. As for running, you don't need to be sprinting the whole ten miles, and you don't need to do it all in one day. If you just do a mile and a half a day, you'll meet your goal. It'll take maybe 20 minutes of your time.

In order to stop procrastinating, it's useful to break down tasks into small, obtainable goals. If you have some sort of multifaceted project, don't just try to do it all at once. Look for things you can measure; send ten emails to clients today, collect five sources for preliminary research. Make a game out of your work. People naturally feel good about themselves if they can see the progress they have made. It's part of the reason why games like World of Warcraft or Runescape are so successful; these games are built around making the player feel constantly rewarded, through level-ups, tasks, learning new skills, defeating a boss, etc. Even if these tasks can be monotonous, it doesn't feel that way because the player is positively reinforced. You can do the same with your work as well. If you write 500 words, then reward yourself with a nap. If you eat a serving of vegetables a day for a week, maybe get yourself some pizza or ice cream. If you finish your project, go out for drinks with some coworkers. The human brain is wired for rewards. Casino slots are addictive just because of the potential for a reward; you don't even have to win all that much in order for it to be addictive. Even if we are intelligent creatures, we are not immune to the effects of operant and Pavlovian conditioning. In fact, because we are intelligent, we are quicker to establish causality than are other animals. We can understand almost intuitively that pulling a lever makes the slots spin. In the same way, we understand that the water level rises if we drop ice in our water glass. Humans naturally attribute causation to pretty much anything, even if it doesn't exist. We can use this tendency to our advantage. Set up your own causality; if I write 500 words, then I'll make myself some coffee.

At this point, you might be asking yourself if setting up rewards for yourself contradicts the idea of enjoying the task for what it is. Well, there's a yes and a no. Yes, if the *only* thing that causes you to perform the activity and to stop procrastinating is the reward, then you have fallen into reward oriented thinking. The answer is no if you are using the reward as a congratulation for meeting your goal. You should not *need* a reward for every little thing that you do, but they are a fun and healthy mood booster that can be used to improve productivity when in a pinch. More importantly, however, the end game of rewarding yourself for meeting your small goals is to create discipline, and then, later on, to create good habits.

Overtime, you can start spacing out your rewards to be more and more infrequent. You don't have to reward yourself every time you write 500 words. You'll notice that you can write 500 words pretty easily over time; you've been training the mental muscle to do it with relative ease. Here is the catch: now that you can meet your goals easily, you can even do it on days where you are feeling unmotivated. The essence of discipline is following your routine, even if you don't want to.

If you become accustomed to meeting your small goals on a daily basis, let's say you've been writing 500 words a day for two months straight, eventually, you will feel strange whenever you *don't* write 500 words a day. Even without the prospect of a reward, not meeting your goals will make you feel uncomfortable. At this point, your actions become a habit; working towards your long term goals becomes as natural as breathing. We want to have a routine that we can rely on.

Routine is beneficial for your brain. Not only does it make processing information more efficient, but it also can help to reduce anxiety and improve focus. Many people are anxious and overthink things because they do not really know what they are going to be doing from day to day. They tend to panic about what they should be doing because they need to think ahead about it. Routine gets rid of the need to think ahead about everything. If you know that you will make progress by sticking to your routine, then you don't have to overthink when it comes to finding ways to make progress. Having a routine is also a great time saver. As you get accustomed to your routine, you can go through it more quickly and feel less exhausted in doing so. This opens up time and energy for other things, whether that is going to the gym, getting more sleep, or cooking a meal for yourself rather than eating out. Having a routine is likely to make other aspects of your life healthy, and you'll have more resources available for your personal enjoyment and benefit.

Let's keep this in mind: we are only human. We require things like sleep, we need food, and we need to take care of yourself. No matter how disciplined you are, you cannot just push through exhaustion at every moment. Sometimes you'll just hit a wall. You might be focused on the task, and you might not be particularly tired, but you simply cannot get any work done. You will probably begin to overthink at this point, with intrusive thoughts of self-doubt questioning why you cannot get any work done. Maybe you have writer's block. At this point in time, you absolutely need to take a break. There is no way around it; just trying to brute force your way through will lead to greater exhaustion and poorer results. Take some time to yourself. Take a day off if you can. Seriously, take a day off, you deserve it. Meditate. Relax. Go to bed early. Go to a spa. Go for a run or to the gym. Do something, anything, to get your mind off of your work. Let yourself *not* focus for a little bit. Mental exercise is taxing. Think about it in terms of physical exercise; it's impossible to run constantly, so at some point, you have to rest. Let your brain take a rest too.

Taking a break can actually lead to some of your best ideas. Even if you are not consciously thinking of your work, chances are, your unconscious mind is doing some of the heavy liftings. Inspiration is a valuable tool at your disposal, even if you can't rely on it all the time. By relaxing, you can sometimes gain valuable insight to a problem; you start to think outside the box, or something you see or hear gives you something important to think about. It's not uncommon to produce some of your best work after taking a break.

Chapter 4: Getting Rid of Anxiety - Meditation and Other Practices

Most people are anxious about something. It could be about social interactions, getting an assignment in by a certain due date, or even just a general feeling of worry without any particular object. Anxiety is strange because it tends to manifest when you least want it to. Anyone who's experienced anxiety knows that it's difficult to work when you are feeling anxious. And because you can't get any work done due to anxiety, you just end up feeling even more nervous. It's a vicious cycle, in which the person gets caught up in repeated and unhealthy feelings of self-doubt, poor performance, and a general sense of nastiness and uncertainty which can never be comfortable.

There are a number of ways in which people can reduce their anxiety. Starting with the most obvious, therapy is something that everyone will benefit from. If you believe you have a general anxiety disorder or any of the numerous anxiety disorders which exist, the best thing you can do is seek help. Therapists are trained clinicians who will help you, and you shouldn't feel ashamed or weak for going. If you really need it, you can be prescribed medication to reduce anxiety, and you shouldn't feel ashamed for taking medication either. It does not define who you are or what you can accomplish as a human being. The stigma around therapy has certainly declined in recent years, with the practice seeing more and more clientele across all walks of life. We are finding more and more that mental health issues can be managed, and we are getting better at diagnosing and recognizing when these problems occur. Serious issues with anxiety and mental health require serious help; take it if you can get it.

We recognize, of course, that not everyone has the resources available to them to seek out treatment from a trained professional. The fact is, going to therapy requires time and money, as does medication. Those who rely on work where they are paid by commission or through the amount of work that they do likely do not have the time or energy to go to therapy, even if they are afflicted by serious anxiety. Additionally, there needs to be a good therapist in your area. Those who live in rural areas are unlikely to have a therapist in their hometown, and so they would need to drive for miles in order to see one, further adding to the time and energy cost.

Fortunately, there are good options available if you lack the resources required to go to therapy. Meditation is one such option. Meditation in and of itself is a broad category, and there isn't one proper way to do it. The commonality across all of the different types is the practice of being able to control your wandering mind; some people call it "calming the monkey mind." We mentioned before that anxiety can be caused by a number of things; those who are anxious tend to worry quite a bit about the future or ruminate about the past. If your mind has nothing else to do, it will often wander off in these directions. Meditation is the practice of centering your mind and existing in the present moment.

One basic way to begin meditation is to focus on the breath. Relax, close your eyes if you feel like it, and get yourself into a comfortable position. Start taking deep breaths in and out through your nose. Start to count; breathe in for two seconds, hold it, then breathe out for four seconds. Do that ten times. Breathe in for three seconds, hold it, then breathe out for six seconds. Each time you do so, feel yourself breathing more deeply each repetition. Don't just suck it all into your chest. Bring the breath lower, into your stomach, diaphragm, and even your back. Feel your lower ribs expand outward. Breathe in for four seconds, hold it, then breathe out for eight seconds. Get into a rhythm. Let this breath feel natural; you don't even need to strain. Keep your focus on your breath.

You'll notice during this process that your mind will deviate from the breath. You might start thinking about some projects you need to do. Try to catch yourself when you do so, but don't beat yourself up about it. Just by beating yourself up about *not* focusing on your breath, you further intensify the lack of focus. Be aware of your inner experiences, but do not judge them. Each time your mind wanders, remind yourself about your breath. Let the wandering thoughts pass through your mind, like a wave. Once in a while, you won't be thinking about *anything* at all; you'll simply be in the moment. These experiences usually only last fractions of a second, since you'll suddenly realize that you aren't thinking about anything, breaking the spell.

When you first start to meditate, you may only be able to maintain absolute focus on your breath for a few seconds at a time, maybe less. This is completely normal. A common misconception about meditation is that it's a passive process when it's not. It can be difficult, and even tiring to focus for an extended period of time on something as simple as breath. Meditation is a lifelong practice. It can take weeks, months, or even years to see cognitive improvement as a result of the practice. There's a reason why there are whole monasteries dedicated just to meditation. I can guarantee that it does get easier. Over time, you'll have less difficulty keeping focus, and you'll be able to practice for extended periods.

If you have difficulty meditating by yourself, it may be beneficial for you to try a guided meditation. Many health centers provide classes led by an experienced meditator. There are also a number of mobile apps or even just free YouTube videos, which will take you through meditation at a slow and easy pace. Additionally, some practitioners find it difficult to maintain focus on the breath and will choose other things to direct their attention towards. It could be a sensation; some common ones are the sensation of air around the body or the feeling of the weight of your body. Some people choose a mantra which they repeat either vocally or subvocally. Some people focus on an action (or a lack of action), such as trying to keep your eyes completely still. Some people simply count as high as they can. The point is, try to find something that works for you. Meditation practice is highly personal.

The fascinating thing about meditation is the benefits one receives even while not practicing. While meditation can be a valuable tool in the moment anxiety through a short meditation session, frequent meditation practitioners experience less frequent bouts of anxiety and can better regulate their emotions. They have an easier time maintaining focus *in general* as well, meaning no matter the topic, they can keep their attention on it.

Meditation isn't for everyone; it's not always enjoyable, and it's hard to see any immediate benefits from it. For some people, sitting alone with your thoughts for twenty minutes at a time can lead to anxiety. Luckily, there are other options available that reduce anxiety.

Journaling is a valuable tool for understanding where anxiety is coming from. There are two ways to do it: (1) When you are having a bout of anxiety, write down how you are feeling, and what is going on around you. It's important that you express just what it is that's going on in your mind. If you're feeling worthless, write it down. If you are feeling overwhelmed, write it down. If you are feeling disconnected from the world, write it down. It is often a challenge just to understand yourself and the emotions which you experience. Putting feelings into words turns the feelings into something concrete. It puts you in a position of power over the feelings; once your feelings are known, they're not so scary. Option (2) involves journaling after the fact, usually making your journaling part of a daily routine. If you've felt anxious during the day, then before you go to bed, write down everything that happened that day. Eventually, you'll have a collection of journal entries, all detailing bouts of anxiety and the events surrounding them. That's when you can start to pinpoint similarities across anxious bouts. Usually, it's only a couple of things that cause anxiety. Maybe you get anxious when you are faced with the prospect of meeting someone new, or when you need to step out of your comfort zone. Maybe you get anxious if you still have work to do. By recognizing what causes your anxiety, you can figure out how to avoid or alleviate it. If you find out you get anxious whenever you have to talk to strangers, you can practice some method of calming yourself down before a conversation, or maybe you can create a routine that you don't have to stress over.

Here's another possibility with journaling: just write down every thought that you have. It doesn't matter how silly, or ridiculous any of these thoughts may be, just write them down. Do this for as long as you please, an hour, a day, or what have you. Once you've finished, go back a look over your thoughts. You'll probably find three things: (1) Not a lot of the thoughts make sense or are connected in any way. They probably are just reactionary measures to something in the environment or are completely random that pop out of nowhere, like a song that is stuck in your head. (2) A lot of the thoughts are negative. That's normal. After all, it's things like fear and negativity, which allowed our ancestors to survive, so it makes sense that our brains are more reactive to and produce more negative thoughts. It's important to understand that these negative thoughts are normal and that you aren't abnormal for having them. What is important is how you learn to respond to and deal with these negative reactions, and to take them for what they are, which is some randomly produced sequence coming from your brain. (3) Many of our thoughts are repetitive. There isn't a whole lot of spontaneity in the content of our thoughts, and quite a few of them are mundane. That's normal too. On the whole, people are fairly boring and uninteresting.

Another option is to engage in healthy self-analysis. Healthy is a keyword here. It's easy to get caught up in disparaging yourself about the little things, and this only exacerbated through anxiety. It can help to have a friend nearby to tell you if you're exaggerating the negatives, which you probably are. A common technique for self-analysis is called "fact-checking." In short, all you are doing is figuring out if your self-assessment is accurate. Let's say you have the thought, "I am a horrible person." You probably aren't, but nonetheless, it's invasive enough to cripple your self-esteem and to create unhealthy habits. Get out a sheet of paper and list the things you have done that make you think you are a bad person. Chances are, this list is pretty small. On the other side of the paper, list all of the reasons *not* to believe that you are a bad person. It could be anything; it could be a good deed that you've done in the past, it could be an assignment that you did well, it could even just be a compliment that you've received. After you've done this, there's still a good chance that you have negative thoughts. The list may generate some other negative thoughts, such as, "I don't deserve the compliment that I received." That when you repeat the process. List out why you think you don't deserve the compliment and list out why you think you do. After this time, you get the thought, "well, maybe they're just pretending to like me." Then you try to figure out what's more likely: (a) they actually like you, or (b) they're involved in some sort of conspiracy where your parents hired him to make you feel good. Option (a) is a bit more probable than option (b). If you repeat this process enough times, you'll realize that most, if not all, of the negative thoughts you have just, aren't true. And if some of the negative thoughts have *some* truth to them, then you can use them as a catalyst for self-improvement.

There's an additional benefit to this sort of self-analysis; once you've followed through on it, you can start to work on cognitive restructuring. You can identify the sorts of mental distortions that you engage in. Let's say you have the constant recurring thought that you are a bad person, but through fact-checking, you've come to realize that this isn't true. What do you do now? You try to figure out *why* it is that you have this thought. Maybe you have a warped sense of what it means to be a good person. Maybe you have far too high expectations of yourself. Maybe you compare yourself to other people too much. There could be any number or combination of reasons; what's important is that you identify them.

The last thing that it's important to talk about in this chapter is maintaining your body. We can boil this down to three main points: water, exercise, and sleep. All of these things are necessary for living a healthy lifestyle, and all of these things are interconnected. We have to remind ourselves that our body's physical state will directly affect our mental state. If your body isn't feeling good, there's a high chance that your brain isn't feeling good either, leading to stress and anxiety. Stresses aren't just mental; many are physical in nature.

You probably learned in elementary school that the body is primarily composed of water. At an intuitive level, then, it makes sense that the thing that needs to be put into our body most is water (technically, water is second most important, next to oxygen, but we've already talked about meditation, and you can't really stop yourself from breathing). Though the body averages out at about 60% water, there are two parts that have a much higher content of water: your blood, which is about 90% water, and your brain, which is about 75% water. As one might imagine, these are two critical systems for your body. Drinking water does a number of things, physiologically speaking. One is that it makes you feel more active; drinking water increases the activity of your sympathetic nervous system. This is the system that is responsible for responding to external stimuli, particularly dangerous external stimuli. It is the fight or flight reaction that we have when one experiences fear. This raises how much energy we expend, which in turn raises our metabolism, and can lead to things like easier weight loss when paired with proper diet and exercises. It is also important for helping to flush toxins from your body; why do you think people need to drink water to prevent hangovers?

If you are reading this now, chances are you are dehydrated. The word dehydrated is often misused; it is not the Hollywood depiction of a person out in the desert for weeks at a time drinking only cactus juice. Dehydration occurs in much less serious forms, and can even be common if a person is used to not drinking water. Mayo Clinic suggests that the average man needs to drink between 15 and 16 cups of water per day and that the average woman should drink between 11 and 12 cups of water per day. To put this in perspective, this is about eight glasses of water a day, if the glasses are 8 ounces each. This is at a minimum. Other factors will influence if you need to drink more, including how hot the weather is, and if the person has been exercising. Simply put, people need to drink a lot of water, probably more than they think they need too. The issue is, people tend to substitute other drinks in the place of water; this includes things like coffee, milk, juice, and soda, which, while composed primarily of water, do not offer the same hydration benefits as pure H2O. Caffeinated drinks such as coffee and soda are specifically troublesome because of the caffeine content. Caffeine acts as a diuretic, leading to more frequent urination and more water loss, meaning you have to drink more water as your system flushes it out. That's not to say it's not a good idea to have a morning cup o'Joe. Just be aware of the effects that it is having on your body, and make sure you make up for the water loss by drinking more water.

Exercise has been highly touted as one of the best ways to get rid of anxiety, and for a good reason. Exercise has a number of physiological effects, most of which have been described in detail. Let's begin with the long term, hard to notice effects.

Exercise provides a number of long term health benefits. Unless you are suffering from severe or debilitating physical abnormalities, there is almost no excuse not to be exercising on a consistent basis. There are the obvious benefits that exercise provides; exercise, as the average person may find, makes you better at exercise. If you run, you will get better at running. If you lift weights, you will get better at lifting weights. If you swim, you will get better at swimming. This, so much, is to be expected. If you do something repeatedly, you will get better at it. There isn't much of an argument against it. Sometimes, this can be beneficial for its own purpose. If you genuinely enjoy running, then it makes sense for you to run more and with better quality. If you are a weight lifter, then it makes sense for you to want to lift more weights at a more consistent time regimen and to increase the weight. You do not need to justify doing these things when doing them seems to be its own reward. In fact, doing things for their own reward is a mark of autotelic experiences, i.e., doing things just because you enjoy them. There does not always need to be an end in regard to the thing that you are doing. As mentioned previously, sometimes you just want to do things because you enjoy them. The autotelic experience is often healthy and is the most important aspect of one's life.

Not everyone needs to exercise just because they enjoy exercise. For instance, I absolutely hate running. If I had the option to, I would never do it. It is horrible, lung burning action that should never be endorsed by anyone for its own sake at any time. In fact, if I hear someone say that they enjoy running, I just assume that they are lying. That is how much I hate it. Nevertheless, I do, in fact, and against all the odds, run. It goes against every fiber of my being, but I do do it. Why? Because I know it's good for me. There is something inherently healthy about doing something this you know is good for you, even though you know you hate it. It is another aspect of self-discipline; doing something that you know is good for you to do even if you do not necessarily like doing it. If you hate eating vegetables, you should still discipline yourself into doing so. Make eating vegetables palatable, but do not avoid it altogether, as it is an important part of maintaining one's diet.

Of course, discipline is not the only reason that I run. I run because I have a goal in mind, even if being a good runner is not a direct part of that goal. For instance, I have a broad goal of staying in shape. There's a difficulty in this goal. Staying in shape can mean quite a number of things. It can mean being able to lift a large amount of weight, it can mean being able to run a mile in a certain amount of time, it can mean running a certain amount of miles without stopping, or it can mean doing a certain amount of pushups within an allotted time frame. Personally, these things don't really matter to me. I don't have a *specific* goal in mind. In order to feel good about myself, I don't need to do exactly 50 pushups without stopping, or I don't need to be able to run a mile in under 6 minutes. I just need to feel good about myself, whatever my criteria for that may be. For example, it could be the case that I have never been able to do more than twenty pushups at a time for my entire life. I could be overweight or simply unsatisfied with my current lifestyle. I decided one day to change something significant about me. Maybe I want to lose weight, or build muscle, or have a more attractive physical appearance (whatever that means). Does being able to do twenty push-ups really make a difference to those goals. Well, yes and no. Being able to do twenty push-ups may be a benefactor in reaching my long term goals; they may contribute to my success or be an inherent part of my goal. If my goal is to get in shape, then I may not have it as part of my goal to be able to do twenty push-ups, Sure, if I *were* in shape, then I would be able to do twenty push-ups, no problem, but that is not my long term goal. Being able to do twenty push-ups is not indicative of overall success or indicative of what I want to achieve. I need other sorts of standards that, when combined, better indicate if I have been able to achieve what I wanted to achieve. I want to stay in shape. That means I want to be able to do twenty push-ups at a time. It also means that I want to run a mile in less than six minutes, or do ten pullups, or do any number of things. Here is a general concept: long term goals can never be just one short term goal. They need to be something that involves component parts and something which you can measure on a number of bases. Let's face it; even if you don't like running, it is good for you. I, for instance, recognize all of the benefits of running and recognize that running is imperative to my long term goal of staying in shape. Unfortunately, I still will not run unless I have some other goal, which I genuinely enjoy in mind. For instance, I play rugby, and if possible and if fates allow, I will play rugby until the end of my days, barring some sort of serious injury or necessary lifestyle change, which requires that I stop playing. Running is a necessary part of the game, whether I like it or not. If I want to be good at rugby, I need to be good at running, more or less. I'm concerned about how well I can run even though I don't enjoy the activity in and of itself. If you can, transform the activity that you hate into something that you enjoy. Think about how you can use a certain activity for something in your career or hobby, If you are practicing weightlifting, maybe you are thinking about how you can more efficiently move your packages or mail if you are working in a warehouse. Be creative with your applications.

So, even if you hate exercise, and even if you can find no reasonable application to your job or anything else in your life, you can and absolutely should still do it. Exercise isn't only applicable to the specific skill sets of the thing which you practice, it is generalizable to the things which you don't even think about, and indeed, can improve your mood, emotion, and overall health. Let's use running as an example once again. Let's say you hate running. Most people do. If offered the opportunity to stay inside, most people would rather than venture out onto the hard concrete. That's okay, and in fact, is fairly typical for the average person. By some miracle, you begin to run, against all volition. Here are the biological facts:

(1) It will be difficult. If you are not in the habit of running weekly, not to mention daily, running will be challenging. You will hate the process, at least at first. Your lungs will be burning, and your legs will be hurting,

and your chest will be thumping. Overall, there will be absolutely nothing enjoyable about the experience.

(2) At some point, all of this misery will be enjoyable, or, at the least, sustainable. For a little bit, maybe after running or a half-mile or a mile or so, something will vanish. You will stop thinking about the pain. You will just sort of accept the fact that things hurt and move on with it. You will understand that your discomfort is only temporary, and so most of the things you hate will just fade away. In reality, you'll still be hurting; you'll just be so accustomed to it that you won't notice any of it. Pitter patter. Step and step and step. It doesn't matter. It hurts, but there's really nothing there. Maybe you're thinking about the trail ahead of you, particularly if you are going off-road, and you need to avoid all of the stumps and twigs and roots which can trip you up, or maybe you're just focused on the next day's activity. It doesn't matter in the long run.

(3) After you've run, you'll come to a strange conclusion. Somehow, the amount of pain that you have gone through does not outweigh the strange feeling of enjoyment that you have gotten because of your run. This phenomenon is colloquially called a runner's high. Let's look at this from an evolutionary perspective. First of all, the human species is pretty weak. If you compare our human race to something like a lion or a gorilla, there is almost nothing we can do in terms of pure physical prowess. Luckily, this isn't the definitive human characteristic. We don't

really muscle out our competition; we don't even need to out brain them, most of the time. The earliest form of hunting in humans is known as persistence hunting, and it is not anything fancy or cool. In fact, from the perspective of the prey, it is certainly terrifying. Persistence hunting is as basic as you can get; a human spots a deer out in the wilderness. The human doesn't have a bow and arrow, or a spear, or any sort of long-range weapon with which he could kill the deer. All he has is his bare body and hands, with which he knows that if he has the deer in his grasp, he could kill it with his stone knife or his ability to choke the deer with his opposable thumbs. Either way, there is an immutable fact that he actually needs to catch the deer in order to kill it. So what's a starving human to do? He runs after it. Maybe this sounds ridiculous to you. But let me ask you a question. How far do you think you could run if it were a do or die situation. Chances are, you could run pretty far. At least a marathon, if not more, I would imagine. You don't actually need to run fast. No matter how fast you run, you will never outrun a quadrupedal deer. In terms of biology, they have you beat. Things that run on four legs will always be faster than things that run on two legs. I cannot out sprint a deer, and I never will be able to. But, I will be able to outrun it. Bipedalism has given us a particular gift; over a large distance, we can keep track of most things. Bipedalism is incredibly efficient. Humans can basically run as far as they want without major repercussions. Not only are we bipedal, but we sweat. We can cool ourselves off in hot climates. We are smart. We can delay gratification for a larger payoff. We can work in groups. We do not have to run every day; we can have other people run to capture prey for the greater good of the tribe. All of this culminated in one thing; it is very bad to have to outrun a human. From the animal's perspective, they are faced with something that never gives up on chasing them, that can thrive even in the hottest of climates, and that if they do seem to tire, another one takes their place. Persistence hunting was based around a very simple concept; outlast your prey. If you can do that, they will tire, and you will capture it and eat it. It doesn't matter how long it takes; eventually, the human will catch up.

We know then that being able to run is highly advantageous for survival. It was basically necessary that you could do it. It makes sense then that your brain and body would similarly adapt, and it did so in the following. Here is the essential question: how do I reward running, even if there is no survival pay off? That is, there are instances where running will not lead to rewards. Sometimes, you'll lose track of your prey, or maybe there will be inclement weather, or maybe you'll run into a predator yourself. You still need to make sure that your body runs. The answer is, make sure that it feels good for your body to run. Whenever you run, or whenever you exercise in general, your body releases endorphins. These are the "feel good" brain chemicals. They're important for things like emotion regulation, stress management, and pain reduction. They're some of the things that keep you running when you don't really want to. They produce the runner's high, and available tools for stress relief and anxiety release.

Exercise, in addition to making you feel good at the moment, has lasting effects afterward. There are obvious ones like building muscle and making your heart more efficient. You change your body composition and become more efficient in your movements. These are good things in and of themselves. Most people just genuinely enjoy the physical benefits.

There are also a number of psychological benefits to exercise. Those who exercise frequently tend to have higher self-esteem, especially when it comes to their bodies. They are typically more satisfied with their daily routines, have improved mood and energy, and are better at coping with stress. They also have a better sense of their physical abilities, which is important for building confidence in one's body.

The last thing this chapter will discuss is sleep. We live in a culture where we seem to pride ourselves on how little sleep we get. If you are only sleeping four to six hours a night, that is taken as a sign that you are working you hard, keeping your nose to the grindstone, and doubling down on meeting your deadlines. Here's the reality: if you are only sleeping that much, the rest of your day is likely not dedicated solely to working. You are probably up on your phone in bed watching youtube videos. Poor sleep is likely a side effect of poor time management and poor discipline. Even if you are working 70 hours a week, that means you are working 10 hour days, assuming you are not taking a day off. That's 14 hours a day leftover for other activities. At least seven of those hours should be dedicated to sleeping, which means that you have 7 hours available for eating and recreation. For most people, lack of sleep is a reluctance to give up any more of your free time, which is certainly understandable. The work culture in which we currently exist has more than a little role in accepting the blame. Frankly speaking, it is an unhealthy culture.

Most people are willing to sacrifice sleep because they are unaware of just how important it is. After all, on the face of it, it just seems like you are knocking yourself unconscious for a couple of hours. How does that seem valuable in comparison to the amount of work you could get done in that time?

The value of sleep cannot be understated. Let's first talk about the effects that sleep deprivation has on your body and mind. They include issues with memory, mood, and focus, which obviously isn't great if you are trying to be efficient in getting your work done. You become more prone to anxiety and depression. Additionally, lack of sleep makes it more difficult to practice anxiety-reducing techniques such as meditation, journaling, and self-analysis. All of these things require focus. Physiologically, lack of sleep weakens your immune system, and can make you more susceptible to unhealthy weight gain or weight loss, and can even increase your risk of diabetes. In short, not sleeping makes it extremely difficult for your body to maintain homeostasis. Your body goes out of whack.

Let's try to understand sleep a bit. There are two types of sleep: the first is called REM sleep, or Rapid Eye Movement

Sleep. Your eyes are rapidly flickering, even if you aren't aware of it. This is the period of sleep where you dream. The other broad category of sleep is Non-REM. Non-REM sleep can be broken down into three more stages. The first is pre-sleep. In this stage, you are shifting over from wakefulness to sleep. Your brain waves begin to slow down. This is the stage you are in when you begin to "drift off" during the day. The second stage is light sleep. Your body and brain relax more, you stop moving as much, you have a lower body temperature, and your eyes stop moving as well. In this stage, you are easy to wake. The third stage is deep sleep. This stage of sleep is the most important. Your body is the most relaxed, and your brain is the most "turned off" it can be. You need this type of sleep to make it feel as if you actually slept. It is hard to wake up during the period of sleep. Throughout a night of sleep, your body goes through these stages and back to REM. Each loop through the cycle lasts about 90 minutes. As you sleep more throughout the night, the time spent in each portion of the cycle changes. You spend less time in the deep sleep stage the more time you spend asleep, making a 12-hour sleep binge less efficient than the recommended 7 or 8 hours.

Like everything else, sleeping needs to become part of your routine and habit. It is difficult for many people to fall asleep because they are inconsistent in how they go about it. The easiest way to get to sleep is to try to do it at the same time every night. You have a natural, circadian rhythm; your body operates on a time schedule, and so if you alter the schedule too much, it won't function as efficiently as it should.

There are a number of vital processes that occur during sleep. Recovery is the big one. Contrary to what a lot of people may think, sleep is actually a fairly active process. Your brain is still firing. Your body is undergoing repairs since there is very little strain on it, and your mind gets an opportunity to relax at least a bit. Let's put exercise and sleep together for a minute. When you exercise, you are actually breaking down muscles. After they've been broken down, they need to be built back up in order to get stronger. You've probably had the experience of delayed onset muscle soreness or DOMS for short. It's the aches and pains you get after a hard workout or a day of manual labor. DOMS generally occurs after a night of sleep. Your body is repairing the broken down muscles, leading to tenderness, pain, or stiffness. Even if you don't feel it, your body does need daily repairs. Everyday stresses like walking, or even typing can cause damage; you do not take the time to recover from them. Sleep is the opportunity to recover. Children even growthe most in their sleep.

Sleep is vital for our mental well being, both on the emotional side of things and on the cognitive side of things. We've already mentioned that a lack of sleep can lead to mood swings, anxiety, and depression and that getting a good night's rest will improve emotional regulation. Sleep is also crucial for learning and memory. During sleep, short term memory is consolidated into long term memory, making it easier to remember things over the course of a lifetime rather than needing to do the mental gymnastics required to keep an idea in your head. The difference between short term memory and long term memory is the difference between cramming for a test the day off and taking the time to study multiple nights ahead of the test. Sure, you may be able to get away with it, but you likely will not be able to remember the information on the test after it is over. We need to sleep in order to actually learn how to do things, which means we need to sleep if we want to improve ourselves.

Sleeping at night is obviously important, but a lot of people would benefit from taking naps as well. One product of our modern society is our monophasic sleep; that just means that we tend to sleep in just one session, usually at night. The rest of our time is spent in wakefulness. However, there is evidence to suggest that this may not be natural and that humans may not have only slept that way. Humans used to break up their sleep into two phases a night, something like two, three-and-a-half-hour sessions of sleeping. They might wake up in the middle of the night to do various activities, usually related to keeping themselves or their loved ones safe.

Most people would benefit from naps. Even if we get a good night's sleep, there are times when we experience drowsiness or grogginess throughout the day. The Sleep Foundation suggests that taking a nap serves to alleviate some of the grogginess, providing another way of rejuvenating your mind and body. However, it needs to be done in the correct way. First, the nap should not be too long; they should really only last between 20 and 30 minutes. Any longer can create sleep inertia, actually leaving people more tired than when they first went to sleep. The second thing to be aware of is that you should try to avoid taking a nap too close to your normal bedtime. Doing so can alter your normal circadian rhythm, making it difficult to fall asleep as you normally would for the night. Lastly, be aware of where you are napping. Of course, you want to be comfortable during the duration of the nap, but where you do, it can create habits. One general tip for sleep is to reserve your bed solely for sleeping. If you are on your phone or computer when in bed, it can create a bad habit where your body doesn't expect to go to sleep. We want to program our bodies to go to sleep at certain times and in certain places. Likewise, choosing to nap in a place where you normally wouldn't hardwire your body to feeling tired while being in a particular location, whether that be a room or a certain sofa. It's easy to imagine places where you wouldn't want to fall asleep, such as an office or your car. You don't want to induce drowsiness in those situations.

In any case, naps can be used in a variety of ways to restore health and alertness. Some people are habitual nappers, using the nap as a midday refresh in order to stay alert and efficient in their work. Some people use naps only when they know that they need to stay up later than normal. Lastly, some emergency situations call for naps. Studies show that driving when tired can be just as dangerous as driving when intoxicated, and so using naps can reduce the danger you pose to yourself and others.

Chapter 5: Thinking About Yourself

A lot of this book has been dedicated to understanding your own brain, body, and how they interact with the world to produce overthinking anxiety, and other negative effects. It's also discussed various ways to reduce overthinking and anxiety, all of them centered around you, your actions, and your beliefs about yourself. This chapter continues with this trend, targeting how you should approach thinking about yourself and your place, among others. This chapter is in no way exhaustive. There is almost an infinite amount of literature out there discussing the nature of human beings, the nature of the self, humility, and one's place in the universe. Five thousand words are not enough to fully describe or explain the human experience. Furthermore, the opinions in this section draw from various disciplines, not the least of which include biology, psychology, and philosophy. As with most things, the majority of this chapter will be up for debate. It is, however, informed by recent findings in these disciplines. If nothing else, this chapter will present a *healthy* way of thinking about yourself.

Before we talk about the human person, I'd like to challenge you with a classic philosophical problem called the Ship of Theseus. This problem has to do with identity. There is an old wooden ship that has come into dock for repairs. A couple of the pieces of wood on the hull have begun to rot, so the craftsman creates a copy of the wood that was used previously. For all intents and purposes, when the ship is repaired, it looks and acts nearly identically to before the rotting piece of wood was taken out. Over time, more and more pieces of wood begin to rot, and new ones replace all of those pieces of wood. Eventually, every single piece of wood in the ship is replaced. There isn't a single piece of wood left from the original construction. Here is the question: is this fully repaired ship the same ship as it was before it was repaired? If it is not, when did it change into a new ship?

Generally speaking, there are four possible answers to this question:

(1) The ship is the same ship, even after all of the repairs.

(2) The ship is not the same ship. It became a new ship as soon as all of the pieces were replaced (i.e., when there were no remnants of the original left).

(3) The ship is not the same ship. It became a new ship when some percentage of the pieces (i.e., greater than 0 percent, but less than 100 percent) were replaced/

(4) The ship is not the same ship. It became a new ship as soon as even one of the parts were replaced.

There isn't a truly correct answer to this problem. All of them have their downsides and flaws and weird implications, depending on which you accept. We'll go through them one by one, and I promise you, if you are getting bored reading this philosophical mumbo jumbo, there is a practical pay-off in how we think about ourselves. I promise.

Answer number (1) is strange on an intuitive level. After all, how can it be the same ship even if there are none of the original parts? Sure, it may have the same shape and function as the original ship, and people likely call the ship by the same name. Maybe the ship has the same essence, but it is quite different. There are different trees used in the construction, different nails, different lacquer, etc. Two pencils are not identical to each other just because they have the same properties. Thinking about answer (1) leads us to the following conclusion: something about what the ship is *made* of matters when we are talking about whether something has stayed the same.

Answer number (2) is weird because it basically does not account for any of the time in between the original construction and the full repair. What is so special about adding that one piece of wood which fully changes the material that it changes the identity? What is so special about the last remaining piece of rotting wood that prevents the identity from changing?

Answer number (3) is just far too vague; it barely even counts as an answer, essentially amounting to "you know it's different when you see it." The issue is, what counts as different will vary from person to person, without really an objective way of viewing the change. Do you need to change by 75%? What about 50%? 25%? You can endlessly debate which percentage you need, the benefits and detriments of each one, how you can measure change, etc. Even if you do settle on a number, you can ask another question? What happens to the identity if we keep adding more, or if we take away something? Answer (3) isn't equipped to deal with this.

Answer number (4) is, in my book, the most palatable of the answers, and the answer we will be applying to think about ourselves. Let's think about it conceptually for a bit. We know from looking at the answer (1) that something about what the thing is made of matters in determining its identity. However, identity isn't this unified sort of thing. We can distinguish between something qualitatively being the same, and something *quantitatively* being the same. The argument goes that the boat is actually the same as it was, *quantitatively* speaking. By repairing the boat piece by piece, we haven't really changed what we identify the boat as, numerically speaking. There is still only one boat, a boat that we will still call the Ship of Theseus. However, the boat is certainly different when it comes to its qualitative properties. After all, it has different wood, nails, etc.

Answer (4) is the best of both worlds; it explains why things can be different, yet have the same numerical identity. For example, just because you sharpen a pencil and it loses some of its wood, it does not mean it is not the same pencil. It has just lost some of its qualitative properties. However, answer (4) does have some strange implications. The biggest one, as you've probably noticed by now, is that it implies constant qualitative change. It doesn't matter how little material something loses or gains; it could be mere atoms. As soon as some material or matter is added or subtracted; this becomes qualitatively different. This implication is one I am willing to accept, as the idea of constant change may be beneficial to use as a concept when talking about ourselves.

Without further ado, let's talk about how answer (4) applies to the concept of the self.

When we're talking about *you*, we usually have some semblance of an entity that we can talk about. Generally, it's *you* in the present moment. It's not the *you* of the past, or the *you* of the future. We are talking about whatever *you* are, as you are, right now. If you're reading this, you are probably a human being, a person who experiences things as they come, with some degree of consciousness. If we are to believe our eyes and ears, *you* exist in reality, experience reality, and actively participate in reality. To use some philosophical terms, you are an *agent*; you do things. Some things that you do are good, some things that you do are bad, some things you do are neutral. Some things you do matter, even for the world at large or for individuals others and some things that you do, won't even be noticed, often not even by your own self.

The argument that I am going to advance is that the type of person that *you* are is changing from second to second or moment to moment. It seems reasonable to say that you are a different person from who you were as a baby. You've learned new things, you've gotten much larger, you can speak. The way you fundamentally experience the world now is much different than how you did so as a baby. If it's reasonable to say that you are a different person from who you are when you are a child, then it is reasonable to say that you are different from who you were ten years ago, five years ago, a year ago, a month ago, a week ago, and an hour ago, or a second ago.

For some people, this might be a scary thought. They seem to equate being a different person with not having an identity. That is, I am *not* the same person I was an hour ago, then who am I? That's not quite the argument being made. You can still identify with that person who you were an hour ago, but that does not mean that you haven't changed. You have the same identity but are a different person. What matters is that all of your experiences are connected; you are a constant stream of thoughts and feelings, all causally linked through the past, present, and future. Who you constantly change, the moment to moment thoughts and feelings can change at the drop of a hat. To use a bit more philosophical jargon, you have only changed *qualitatively*. You have not changed *quantitatively*.

One implication of this sort of view is the possibility of reinvention. You can decide how you want to change at every moment, without being concerned about how it will reflect on your past self. Let's say, for example, that a couple of years back, you had some issues with alcoholism. You've managed to seek treatment and were able to overcome it; now you are five years sober, and rarely have a craving for alcohol. You've become a different person, and all for the better. However, you can still identify with that person you were years ago. You can recognize that you have changed on a fundamental level, but your identity remains the same; you have a different qualitative identity, but the same quantitative identity. You are still the same entity, connected to your past through your memory and experiences, but you have a new lease on life. Furthermore, you don't need to deny that your past experiences have played an important role in shaping who you are now. You can take them exactly for what they are; past experiences which affected you when you were a different person, qualitatively speaking. You can critically reflect on who you were in the past. You can examine all of the things which led up to you being you today.

If all of this is true, then we are very lucky. Each passing moment represents a new opportunity to change yourself. You are not trapped by being "a certain type of person." Types of people don't even exist. You simply are who you are in the present. And with that, you can exercise a large degree of control. You can choose how you will act in the present. You can make continual choices to ensure that you have a good life. That begins with understanding the sort of creature that you are.

Even if we can understand this, what is the best way to live a fulfilling life from moment to moment? How can we avoid the mental traps of ruminating about our past or worrying about the future? We've previously touched on meditation, self-analysis, and journaling as ways of dealing with these mental traps, but unfortunately, we can't practice this all the time. At the end of the day, we want to stop anxiety and rumination before they even begin. This means we need to approach our day to day life in a way in which these things are unlikely.

The first thing we can talk about is confidence. Being confident has a number of benefits; those who are confident, i.e., those who believe in themselves are more likely to perform well. It has the opposite effects of self-doubt. If you are confident, you perform better, and that good performance leads to more confidence. Those who are confident tend to be more emotionally stable and better at emotion regulation. Those who are confident handle adversity better, and are not as put down by insults. As stereotypical as it may sound, confidence is, in fact, the key to success, whether we like it or not. This may seem unfair; some people appear just to be born with confidence. Maybe their parents instilled it in them, or maybe they were successful from a young age. Some people are just more naturally confident than others, and will never actually have to work on it. To those people, we say, “good for you!”

For the rest of us, mere mortals, confidence is hard to come by. We tend to be more sensitive to insults than compliments. We could get 100 compliments a day, but the one insult that we get will linger in our mind longer than all of the compliments. If we are confident, it can be ruined just as easily either through some fault of our own, such as a major screw up or by some seriously harsh words. Additionally, it’s hard to be generally confident; that is, confident in all aspects of life. Most people are confident in just a few things, usually, the things that they are good at. A computer programmer may be confident in his ability to write code, but might be less confident during social interactions. Even some professional athletes are confident while competing but seem awkward and shy when they are interviewed by the press.

Like everything we've discussed so far, being confident is a skill, and as such, it needs to be treated as a skill. Skills need practice. However, unlike other skills, it seems like you already *need to be* confident in order to practice confidence; we already mentioned how being confident further creates more confidence. So it's a catch-22; how am I supposed to gain confidence if my own lack of confidence is preventing me from doing so?

Lucky for us, confidence has another unique quality. Confidence is a subjective measure, particular to the individual. It's the same thing as something like happiness or excitement. People can only tell if someone is excited by visual or verbal cues. If they look like they're excited, i.e., they're smiling, bouncing up and down, etc., then we naturally think that they actually are excited. This might not necessarily be true. The person could just be faking it, and we would have no way of knowing. This can be used to our advantage.

You've probably heard of a study where people are told to smile for an extended period of time. The control group is told to hold a neutral or negative facial expression. After about five minutes or so, both groups are surveyed to judge how happy they are feeling. On average, the group that was instructed to hold a smile reported greater feelings of happiness than the neutral or negative facial expression groups. The physical act of forming a smile tricks their brain into feeling happier. We can apply this to building confidence. You've probably heard of the expression "fake it until you make it." If you can't do something, pretend like you can. If you aren't confident, pretend like you are.

Much like the smiling study, pretending you are confident can create a real sense of confidence in the future. People will take it at face value that you *are* confident if you *act* confidently. This may cause them to treat you differently, to respect you more, to look to you for advice. These are the social cues that build your confidence. We can also reuse the idea of visualization. Visualize yourself acting confidently, even if you do not feel that way. Ask yourself, "what can I do or say that makes me appear self-assured?" Then, mentally, practice whatever the answer to that question is. Confidence, for the most part, requires two things: the proper attitude and preparation. Prepare what you will say and do, know it ahead of time, so you don't have to make up too much on the spot. The attitude will come along once you've built a habit of *acting* confident.

The psychological benefits are there as well. If you see yourself acting confidently for a decent amount of time, you might just trick yourself into believing that you are. We can make cognitive dissonance work for us. Most people think that your thoughts and beliefs drive your actions, and this is true most of the time. However, there are instances in which your actions (in this case, acting confidently and boldly) do not derive from true beliefs about yourself. Your mind does not like this; your mind likes when your beliefs and actions line up with one another. If not, you become uncomfortable. For example, let's say you started a job that you didn't really like. Maybe it's just really boring or tedious, but it pays the bills. After some time working there, your boss decides he needs to hire another employee. The potential employee wants to talk to you to get a feel for what it's like working there. Your boss knows that you don't particularly like the job, and he knows that you will tell the potential employee that it is boring if he does not intervene. Your boss offers you a bribe; if you tell the employee that you think the job is fun, then he will give you a paid day off tomorrow. You've had a really stressful day and could really use some time to yourself, so you accept the bribe and tell the potential employee that you enjoy working there. In short, you've lied to the employee about what you actually think, and so your action, i.e., telling a lie, does not align with your true belief. This causes some psychological discomfort; you don't want to be a liar, and you feel cheap at having been bought out to lie by your boss. So what does your unconscious mind do?

Your unconscious mind plays a trick on you: it says, "maybe that job is more fun than I give it credit for. I'm a good person so that I wouldn't lie. If I actually believe that I enjoy my job, then I haven't lied at all." The same thing happens if you start acting confidently. Your brain says, "It's very strange that I am acting confidently right now. How unusual. Maybe I am actually confident. That would explain my actions."

To be sure, this isn't an immediate reaction that your brain has, particularly for ingrained traits like confidence. As with meditation, you won't see benefits right away, at least not any inward benefits. Once again, we want to make the attitude of confidence into a habit. We want our immediate reaction to a challenge not to be one of fear, or doubt, but rather one of self-assuredness. Ultimately, through confidence, we want to cultivate self-efficacy, the idea that no matter how challenging something, maybe, I can work hard and do it.

I'm going to go on a bit of a tangent to talk about poker for a little bit since poker can teach us lessons about attitude. Poker, by nature, is hard to learn, even if you take the time to study and practice. Poker is also attractive because it seems like it could be a get rich scheme to many young players. Most young players are naive; they believe that they can rely on the cards and their own knowledge of statistics to get by. This may work on a lower level; most poker players are fairly bold. If they have something that is close to the best hand, then they will bet high. This isn't a bad strategy. In effect, it amounts to the following line of thought: when you have a good hand, bet high, when you don't have a good hand, bet low (or not at all), and when you have an unsure hand, minimize the losses. This entire strategy revolves around minimizing the amount that you lose, and since in poker, you are primarily playing against other players, the more that you can minimize your losses, the more that you can play. Since most bad players are bad at minimizing your losses, then you end up winning in the lower leagues of poker.

However, once you make it up to the big leagues, it becomes a whole different story; there is a reason why poker tournaments are meant to be held in person and not online. Everyone that makes it to the round table in poker knows the probabilities. It doesn't matter if you know that a 3-pair of kings gives you a 70% chance of winning if everyone else on the table knows it too. On a less skilled table, you could probably get someone to go all-in on your hand, giving you an easy win, but skilled players are not so hasty. They need some sort of convincing. They will see the patterns that you have when you bet. If you have a pattern as simple as "bet when you have a good hand and don't bet when you have a bad hand," then they will see right through you. Knowing probability becomes only a baseline when you enter the pro leagues. Skilled players can still take the pot even if they have a zero percent chance of outright winning the hand if they are good enough at bluffing. If you don't believe me, let's look at a real-life example. Let's say that you are dealt an Ace-Ace hand, with the aces being a spade and a heart. This is about as good as a hand you could get on the draw. If you get an ace on the flop, your win is all but guaranteed unless your opponent gets a flush, or straight, or full house. These things are pretty avoidable. They usually don't occur. Let's say that you are playing to maximize how much you earn. This means that you want to draw people into your hand. If you go all in right away, there won't be anyone to match you, unless they are equally as lucky or just dumb. On average, if you play conservatively, and you don't bully people out, this gives you a 64 percent chance of winning if three people agree to see the flop with you. Now, of course, this flop determines a lot of things. If you see another ace on the flop, you almost automatically win, and you can play the hand according to the table, trying just to maximize profits. But this isn't always the case. Sometimes, you will get a flop that looks like this: King of Hearts, Queen of Spade, 10 of hearts. What do you do then? You still have the best chance of winning. You still have two aces, and with no matching pair on the flop, if you were to reveal your hand right now, nothing could beat you short of a three pair or a straight. However, there may be this thought lurking in the back of your mind. What if your opponent has two hearts? If that's the case, then they would have four hearts on the flop, and they would only need one more heart in the remaining two draws to beat you. That is slightly less than a 50-50 chance, which, if three people are still playing, appears to be less than desirable. A lot of people would get psyched out by this scenario, particularly if there is money on the line.

Let's say that you, confident in your ability to win the round, bet a reasonable amount of money—an amount of money befitting the person having the best possible hand of the round. During the same round of betting, the person across the table from you not only matches the bet that you have but doubles it. What do you do now?

Here are the facts. The likelihood of winning the pot *has not changed*. However, there is still a possibility of someone beating you. Your only job now is to figure out if that person actually has the nuts (i.e.e the best possible hand), or is just trying to swindle you out of your money through a bluff.

You can not rely on probability at this point. The only reason that the person across the table from you is betting as much as they have is that they know the probability of you winning. Here is a strange concept for poker, and for success in general: unless you have a 100% chance of success, a bluffing opposition will be more likely to bet against you. Ironically, the more sure that you are in your hand, the more likely it is that you have small bets put against you. Poker is actually fair in this sense; in poker, you actually have to match the amount of money.

Unfortunately, in real life, this isn't the case. You can actually just make small bets against people who are likely to be successful. One tidbit bit of psychology is that people are more willing to overestimate the probability of good things happening to them than they are willing to accept that bad things are likely to happen to them on a relative scale. And so if you bet a small amount on a bunch of things that people think are unlikely to happen to them, you can make money because the odds will be in your favor.

Anyway, back to poker. So let's say that there is a 60% chance of you winning a poker hand. In your head, you are likely to bump that chance up to 80%, even without your realizing it, and even with the statistical knowledge that this hand has a 60% chance of winning, your emotions intuitively make you *feel* that the probability is higher. So you will be more likely to raise the stakes.

However, at this point, all of this talk of probabilities and statistics are red herrings. You are only distracting yourself from the real issue. Poker isn't you versus a logical computer, or you versus probability, it is you versus another real human being that can calculate probabilities, lie, bluff, and do everything that you can do. As said before, the real question is whether or not you think he or she has a hand that can beat yours. And if you do think they have a better hand than you, do you think that you can get away with bluffing? Let's take a look at what happens if you don't try to answer these questions, only playing by the book through statistics.

The first thing that you notice is that this strategy pretty much just depends on blind luck. If you get good hands, then you will be betting more and winning more. If you are getting poor hands, then you won't be betting at all. You have almost no influence or control over the situation; frankly speaking, a computer could do your job better than you. This isn't the only downside; good players will catch on to your strategy. They will know that if you are betting, you have a good hand and that if you are not betting, then you have a bad hand. They can adjust their own strategy accordingly. They can just choose not to bet if you are betting big, or they can bet big themselves since they know you won't challenge on a bad hand. You become far too predictable, only playing *not to lose* rather than *playing to win*; they lack the confidence to be bold.

The reason why I even mention poker at all is that the mentality you need to be successful in poker is also the mentality you need to be successful in almost anything else unless you are extremely fortunate. To win big in poker, you have to bet big, and you have to be willing to take risks that may put you in some form of danger. You can get by just taking small bets on things that are sure to happen; most people can work a 9 to 5 shift and be reasonably comfy. But if you are reading this book, that might not be what you want. The people that make it big without already being big (i.e., coming from a wealthy family) are the people that take some form of risk.

When I say "make it big," I'm not just talking about money. When I say make it big, I'm referring to the idea of being successful, and success can mean whatever you want it to mean. Part of success is the feeling you get from it. Being successful should be something that is fun, and part of the fun is taking these risks, overcoming it, and being able to say to yourself that you did it.

I'd also like to give one or two more words of caution: just because I say that you need to take risks does not mean you need to make everything a risk, nor does it mean you need to take a risk so big that everything will end up in catastrophe if it doesn't work out. The risks that people in poker take are calculated; they're not just going all-in on every hand, and they are still using the odds to determine their decisions. They can still use concepts like expected value and minimaxing in order to figure out what the most effective course of action will be, and this goes for life as well. Don't take dumb risks; take risks that you think will be worth the payoff.

There are limits to confidence, however. While it's good always to have a confident attitude in how you go about your daily business, it is no replacement for the actual practice of other skills. Confidence should be seen as a bolster to other practiced skills, and can not always be relied on to pull through difficult situations. Just because I'm confident that I will hit a baseball doesn't mean I will, especially if I've never played baseball before. There is a fine line between confidence and foolhardiness. Embarrassing yourself because of foolhardiness can decrease confidence. Confidence should be directed towards your *potential*. Know that you can do anything, but only with the proper time and dedication.

Even if you are confident, other issues can arise. No matter how confident you may be, you might still not be happy. There is no big secret to being happy. What makes someone happy is incredibly subjective; not everyone likes the same thing, has the same values, has the same interests, etc. When it comes to happiness, you need to figure out what works for you. But there are some things that everyone can keep in mind when searching for their own piece of mind.

First things first: it is impossible to be happy all of the time. Sure, you can be happy most of the time, you can learn to be content with what you have, and you can be appreciative of all of the good things that you have come your way. These are all great qualities to have, and they certainly lend themselves to happiness. Even the happiest people are usually just content; they're not ecstatic every waking moment of their lives, but they are rarely dissatisfied with the way things are going. Happiness, or sadness, or anger, for that matter, only exist in opposition with their counterparts. It is really difficult to know happiness, and more importantly, to *appreciate* happiness if you've never been sad. You'll never get anywhere if you get caught up with these negative emotions. Know that they will pass, eventually, and that you can appreciate the happiness all the more because of it.

One peculiar thing about happiness is the tendency of other people's happiness to rob you of your own. We can imagine a little kid who decides to get some ice cream from the school cafeteria. Maybe it's one of those days when the lunch lady hands them out for free. He gets his lunch, eats his ice cream, and is happy. Then, he looks over to the student next to him, and he sees that this student has not one, but two ice creams! The lunch lady must like him more, so she gave him two! Suddenly, the happiness the kid had felt before is diminished by the fact that another student has more than him.

They say that comparison is the thief of joy, and this is absolutely true. People tend to compare what they have to what other people have and get frustrated or upset if what they have is less. Maybe it is some sense of unfairness or injustice. This is why studies have shown that people in poorer countries tend to be happier than people in wealthier countries; there is less of a disparity in income and material well-being in more impoverished countries than there is in more affluent nations. All this goes to show you that it is not what you have that brings you happiness; it is *how you think about* what you have that does.

People must walk the line between being content and appreciating what one has, versus striving for more good things. They must be able to do both. Recognize what you have to be thankful for. Cherish it, don't throw it away just for something shiny and new. But, it can also be bad to just sit on these good things. You can still improve yourself; you can still help more people. You can recognize that you can do more good in the world while still maintaining your own happiness. You don't need to be upset that you don't have more than another person. You also have to recognize that just because someone has more than you, it does not necessarily mean that they are happier than you. Just like you might be doing, they are also doing this sort of happiness comparison. Maybe they're looking at someone who has three ice creams. Maybe that person is looking at the person who has four ice creams. Maybe that person is jealous of the person making the ice cream, and that guy is jealous of the person who owns the store, and that guy is jealous of the person who owns the company, and on, and on, and on. The act of comparison must end with you. You must be content in the knowledge that you can choose happiness, and that if a person is happier than you are, well, good for them. You should not be angry that someone is happier than you. Instead, be happy for their happiness.

Chapter 6: Peak Experiences, Flow State, and Self Actualization

Abraham Maslow wrote about a hierarchy of needs. If you've taken an introductory psychology class, you've probably studied them at least a little bit. The first needs that must be satisfied by people are physiological needs. This includes having food and water, shelter, and other things that are demanded by biology in order to survive. If you don't have these things, it's hard to direct your attention to anything else. If you don't have food, the only thing on your mind will be where your next meal is coming from. Most people in first world countries do not have this problem, except those who are the most vulnerable in society such as the homeless. The second need is safety. People need to make sure that they won't be attacked, and that if catastrophe does strike, they have something to fall back on. A safety net can include things like a place to go in a hurricane, or a rainy day fund if your car breaks down. Those in the lowest echelon of society often struggle to meet these needs. If you are working from paycheck to paycheck, then there is nothing to protect you, financially speaking, from illness or some other sort of emergency. Whether we like it or not, our modern society demands that we have a suitable career and a stable job in order to meet these two fundamental needs.

The third need, right above safety, is love and belonging. Everyone wants to feel like they have a place to go, somewhere that they can call home, people that they can call friends and family. While not so fundamental as food and safety, people with a sense of love and belonging tend to be far healthier, happier, and more successful. There are a number of studies that show that belonging to a strong community can decrease stress and even prolong your life. One study found a correlation between belonging to a church and higher health levels and higher life expectancy. The dynamics of the need will change over the course of a lifetime. As a child, your community will be your parents and your peer group, but as you get older, it will be up to you to pick and choose what sort of community you want to belong to, and/or what sort of community you want to create.

The fourth need is esteem. This need relates to how one views him or herself and includes things like respect and self-esteem. It also relates to how people view you; do they think you are strong, status worthy, and a good role model? Those with a high fulfillment of this need feel a sense of accomplishment in what they have done, and strive to do more with their lives. Those with high esteem are free to choose what they want to do.

Esteem is a strange criterion in that esteem can be variable depending on the circumstances. People will have higher self-esteem in some areas of life than in others, with the higher esteem coming into place in situations where the individual is comfortable, or where they are highly skilled.

People may have high self-esteem when around friends and family, but low self-esteem around strangers or people who are hostile towards them. Likewise, they might feel good about themselves when they are doing something that they like doing. If they are a skateboarder, they may feel better about themselves in a skatepark.

The last need, which is rare and difficult to achieve, is self-actualization. This need is difficult to describe, as it is sort of an ineffable and intangible quality. Those who reach self-actualization have reached the limits of their potential. They have fully satisfied the needs under them, and in doing so, have sort of transcended themselves. They are less concerned with the good of themselves, and more concerned with what they can do to make a positive impact on the world. Self-actualizers are the pinnacle of morality, the absolute do-gooders who have made a profound and important difference in the world. Self-actualizers are the people like Ghandi, or Martin Luther King, who take on a role that goes beyond the status of humanity. They are an icon and symbol of something greater than themselves, someone who conjures up emotion, sentiment, and history just by hearing their name.

Self-actualization is the most that humanity can be, and the path towards it is never easy or straight forward. But it is something that people naturally strive for; who doesn't want to live up to their full potential and make a positive impact on the world? The hope of this book is that we can help you meet these needs and get closer to self-actualization. This book can't really help with physiological or protection needs; unfortunately, you'll have to figure that one out by yourself. But the previously mentioned techniques and practices can help with satisfying love and esteem.

Maslow also wrote about peak experiences. Peak experiences are those rare moments in time where you feel completely whole, at peace with the world, and part of something that is larger than yourself. You often gain insight into the nature of the world and the nature of being. It is pure bliss. Some might consider them to be a religious experience.

Unfortunately, it's extremely difficult to produce or replicate these peak experiences through our own volition. Most of these peak experiences are reactionary; they often occur in response to something awe-inspiring or sublime, whether that be some event, a piece of nature, or some spectacular person. You just need to be lucky enough to be in the right place at the right time. However, self-actualized people are more likely to have or interpret these sorts of experiences since they don't need to focus on their physiological or psychological needs. They can just exist in the present moment, without consciously thinking, just absorbing the sensations before them.

We can also talk about the flow state. Flow state is an interesting phenomenon which is certainly more common than these sorts of religious peak experiences. Mihaly Csikszentmihalyi is the eminent psychologist who first operationalized the flow state. He and his colleague, Jeanne Nakamura, have conducted a number of studies over the past 30 or so years attempting to understand the phenomena and to break it down into its component parts. If you have a greater interest in the topic, I would highly recommend that you read their essays, *The Concept of Flow* and *Flow Theory and Research*.

Both are highly informative about the causes and effects of flow and go into great detail about phenomenal flow state qualities.

In short, Nakamura and Csikszentmihalyi summarize the flow state as the mental state one has when one is both optimally engaged with a task and optimally performing/fulfilling that task. When an individual is optimally engaged, all of his or her attentive resources are fully dedicated to the completion of the task. If we refer back to chapter 2, this means that both System 1 and System 2 processes are fully engaged. Optimal performance implies that the individual is performing the task-relevant functions to the best of their abilities; they do not need to be perfect, merely doing their best. This is a relief since it means that people do not need to be professionals in their field in order to enter flow state; anybody can do it, so long as the conditions are correct. Nakamura and Csikszentmihalyi detail exactly what those conditions are.

The first and most important criterion for entering a flow state is a challenge-skills balance. This means that the task at hand is suitably challenging in reference to one's skills. If a challenge is too easy, then the individual becomes bored. They are not optimally engaged with the task at hand. If the task is too difficult, an individual is likely to become anxious or stressed about their performance, meaning they will not have optimal performance. This criterion explains the phenomena of "clutch players" in sports; we all know that professional athletes are insanely talented, although some are more talented than others. People like Lionel Messi or Lebron James are clearly a cut above the competition and consistently perform at higher levels than the rest of their team or their opponents. Oftentimes, however, it doesn't appear like they are trying until it really counts, as in things like playoffs or championships. Lebron is a notoriously good play-off player, and it's when he performs his best. The challenge has been raised to the point where it matches his skill level, demanding his full engagement, and so he is able to bring out his best.

Sometimes, you will be put into a situation where you can't really control the level of difficulty. For instance, let's say you've started a part-time job as a cashier at a seasonal business. Maybe you started to work at a surf shop or a beach themed department store. When do you think that this type of store would be the busiest? Probably during the summer, meaning if you start your job during June. July, or August, you will be thrown to the wolves in terms of difficulty, especially if you haven't worked as a cashier previously. This can be extremely overwhelming, producing anxiety. You don't have the opportunity to take it slow, learn the basics, and become accustomed to the workflow.

There isn't really a solution to this problem. The only way to begin something new is to practice it in a pressure-free environment. It is difficult to learn under pressure since you are not really focused on improving in any way. You are just focused on getting things done, whatever the cost of doing it may be. You probably aren't improving efficiency, and you are probably making a lot of mistakes along the way. There is only so much you can do to make this situation better.

The first is to ask for help. Having other people around to distribute the workload and to offer advice is sure to make your job easier and less stressful. The other thing is to ask for a shift or a less stressful environment. Maybe try to get a morning shift when there are less people and less responsibility. Sometimes, neither of the options are feasible.

The other option is to practice mentally. Usually, this involves visualizing your activities and your physical practice. If you want to practice shooting a basketball, imagine yourself doing it. Think hard about the feelings and sensations and bodily positions that go into shooting the ball. How are your feet positioned? How deep are you bending your knees? How does the ball feel on your fingers? Try to replicate the feeling of shooting *mentally*, and just as important, *visualize the ball going into the basket*. Replicate the feeling of success. It will help you build confidence. Some studies suggest that this sort of visualization practice actually activates the same neural and motor pathways as a physical practice, although it does so to a lesser degree.

Visualization practice can be used in a variety of ways. It doesn't just need to be used as a repetitive practice for one specific skill or activity. You can use visualization as a precursor to actual success. Some people get anxiety during social interactions, even when it comes to small things like ordering food or talking to their barber. Visualization can help us overcome these small challenges. Before you enter the social interaction, imagine yourself in the situation. What will you say? How will you look? Some people like to think of this from a third-person perspective as if watching themselves on a movie screen. How do you look from the outside? Do you look confident? Attractive? Smart? That's good. Now, repeat the same situation from the inside. Rather than viewing yourself from the third person, just be you in your mind. See the world through your own mind. Make it as rich and detailed as possible. Make it feel real. You have the power to change the perceptions yourself through visualization. After all, it is your imagination that is doing the work. You have the power to alter how others perceive you in your head, and this, in turn, can alter how you choose to act in the real world, which will affect actual perceptions of you.

Nakamura and Csikszentmihalyi list eight other criteria for flow state, with some being more important than others. We will discuss four of them, with a few already being touched on previously in this book.

Research suggests that in order to enter flow state, individuals must have a clear goal in mind of what they want to accomplish and that you must be able to concentrate on the task at hand. In the first chapter of this book, we discussed how overthinking could lead to mental fog. Those who overthink do not have a clear goal in mind when it comes to how they want to solve the task at hand or how they want to be generally successful. As such, in order to meet these criteria, it's important to practice the techniques we've discussed for preventing overthinking. First of all, relax; let your System 1 processes take over what they unconsciously know how to do. Manipulate your environment in such a way as to free yourself from distractions and to allow yourself to focus on the task. If you can't pick out something small to focus on; hopefully, it's something task-related, like a feeling you can use to help you do whatever it is that you need to do. Rely on the routine and the habits that you have built.

To enter flow state, you must also have a strong sense of control of the situation. If you feel as if there is nothing you can do to make a difference, then you have no motivation to do anything at all, and you will not enter the flow state. This is where the confidence-building practice gets in. As mentioned previously, building confidence increases our sense of self- efficacy. The greater our sense of self- efficacy, the more we can feel that our actions matter and make a difference and the more in control that we feel. This criterion is also why flow state can be challenging to achieve when there is ambiguity in where our responsibilities lay, or if we are not in charge of our project or task. Having someone tell you what to do diminishes your sense of control. In group work, or in work where you must follow strict instructions without a lot of agency on the individual's end, try to come to the realization that what you do still makes a difference. You are part of a team, and a team relies on the cooperation of everyone in it in order to be maximally effective. You don't want to be that one person in the group who sits around and does nothing. Think of group work as an opportunity to make a difference to those around you.

Lastly, when in the flow state, the work is autotelic. This is just a fancy way of saying that the work is its own reward—those in flow state value the work that they do for its own intrinsic worth. Chapter 1 discussed how overthinkers tend to engage in reward-oriented thinking rather than task-oriented thinking. Flow state requires task-oriented thinking. It requires that you lose a sense of self- consciousness in order to fully engage with the task. You must be in the present; you cannot be ruminating on the past or worrying about the future.

This last criterion is especially important for long term success. You have to pick and choose what you want to be successful in. Hopefully, it is something that is naturally autotelic and isn't a chore to do. Hopeful, it is also something that can sustain you, not just financially or temporarily, but also spiritually and emotionally. Hopefully, it gives you some sort of purpose in life. This book cannot sort this out for you. But it can guarantee that at some point, you will fail, and that's ok. You aren't going to be satisfied on your first attempt, or your second, maybe even your third. You should take pride in the fact that whatever it is you tried, it didn't work out. That means it wasn't right for you, and that you can better use your potential elsewhere. It's one thing off the checklist. You don't have to return to it, knowing that it won't makeyou happy.

We talk about wanting to be successful in all aspects, and to a degree, it is possible. Obviously, you will be better at some things than others. Success may come easier in one area of life than it does in another, and that's ok. The hope is that we can make the *attitude* that is required for success into a habit and that if you find something that you truly enjoy, that you can spend your time on and fully self-actualize through it. You might call it a vocation. When it comes to vocations, a calling to some duty or task, you may still find it difficult always to be engaged. The best writers in the world, the best athletes in the world, the best at anything in the world, really, will have difficulties. They did not become the best at what they did without effort or practice. In fact, it is exactly because of an insurmountable amount of effort and practice that they got to where they are today. The ability to work hard and to persevere in the face of challenges is a talent in its own right, but it is a talent that can be cultivated and improved. You may be talented in your field; you may possess a natural aptitude for whatever it is that you like doing, but without discipline, motivation, and a continual desire to improve oneself, the path towards success is even more difficult.

Everyone is different in who they are, what they want to achieve in life, and in their potential. There is no journey to happiness or to success that is the same. Ultimately, what makes you happy in the long run will not be the same as anyone else. We also want to distinguish between happiness in the vernacular and happiness in life. When most people use the word happiness, they tend to think of the transient state of emotion. The thing you experience when someone cracks a funny joke, or when you see a baby laughing at you. While this state of emotion is important, it is not the end-all, be all of the human experience. Emotions are definitionally transient, and because of that, they are unsustainable. You just can't have a single emotion all the time. The type of happiness we want to cultivate is the happiness derived from living a good life, whatever that means to you. We also want to distinguish this type of happiness from mere contentment. We can imagine a person who is perfectly content with their being, who just sits around, eats good food, and tries to relax. Maybe they won the lottery. They might be content, but I wouldn't say that they are living a good life. They aren't making many meaningful contributions to the world, and they are not living up to their full potential, which seems like a waste. There isn't anything wrong with their way of living, and I don't want to condemn anyone for living a contented life. I just want to make the finer point that there is often more to existence than contentment. There are always more boundaries to push, more people to meet, more things to try, and more experiences to be had. However, I also don't want to encourage people to sacrifice something good that they have for something that they are very unsure about; at least not without some time taken to reflect on oneself and one's current life. Here is one immutable fact about life and about the type of creatures that we are: we only get one go at things, and because of that, we are always going to miss out on more than we could ever personally experience, which is tragic in its own way, but also liberating in the sense that it reduces the number of things you need to think about. It's easy to fall into the trap of thinking, "I wish I could go back in time," or "I wish things could be different." There are so many what-ifs: what if I was born 100 years ago? What if I went to college? What if I asked that girl or guy out? You only have the ability to choose one option, when there is an infinite number of them available to you. While that may be disappointing, it also means that we have to try to be satisfied with the present choice that we make, to live in the moment, and not to *overthink it*. And, even if you did choose something else than you actually did, that person would not be you, strictly speaking; at least not qualitatively. You are a product of all of your past experiences, memories, tendencies, beliefs, thoughts, knowledge, etc. If you had been born to different parents, you would not be you. If you had grown up in a different area, you would not be you. If you had chosen anything differently, you would not be you. So enjoy who you are in this present moment. There can only be one of you. The only way to find happiness and to be successful is to find meaning in the present.

The other day I watched a movie called It'*s Such a Beautiful Day*. It was simultaneously one of the beautiful, heart wrenchings, but strangely uplifting movies I had had the pleasure to watch, It's a short little animated film about a man who is diagnosed with some form of terminal brain cancer, causing issues with speech, coordination, and most importantly, memory. He began to have troubles, not only remembering who he was in the distant past but also what he did five minutes ago. There's a scene in the movie where our main protagonist gets home from the hospital. He steps outside, thinks to himself, "it's a pretty nice day outside," and decides to go for a walk. He takes a lap around his neighborhood before coming inside once more and promptly forgetting the walk he just took. Once again, he steps outside, thinks to himself, "it's a pretty nice day outside," and then goes around the neighborhood for a second time. This cycle repeats itself maybe three or four times more before the scene ends. While it may be depressing at the surface level, this scene, and the movie as a whole, is making a nuanced point about being able to find meaning in the small moments that the present provides. Despite everything that may be happening to you, whether that be sickness or even the possibility of death, there is still the ability to find and make meaning in the present. Even if you are sick, there may be a nice day outside. Even if you are sad, maybe your friends have come to visit you. Even if you are broke, there are still people that love you.

The reason I mention that movie is because of the challenges that people face during the road to self-actualization. It isn't an easy path, and there will be roadblocks, failures, and people who do not want you to succeed for whatever reason. During those times, it is important that you take a moment to stop and smell the roses. Appreciate the beautiful day that it is. Appreciate yourself for who you are. Meditate, take a nap, journal for a little while. Use what you know, and hopefully, what you have learned from this book, to prevent yourself from overthinking. Let yourself have fun and be fun. We want to improve ourselves, but we don't need to try to do it all the time. We can get burnt out on our own improvement. Take a second to reflect on just how far you have come. Rest up, let yourself go for a little bit. You need to do everything in moderation, which includes doing things in moderation. Treat yourself to something, binge watch a Netflix series, or just sit down with a book. Listen to a podcast, chat with your friends, call your mom. You do not need to be so serious all of the time. If you are happy, let yourself be happy. Don't ruin a good moment just for the sake of trying to do better.

One final note on the nature of success. Success is what you make of it. You have to set your own standards for success. What one person calls a success may be deemed a failure by others. What matters is not what others think; what matters is what you think. Remember to set small goals for yourself. If you haven't reached the pinnacle of all human possibilities in whatever it is you want to achieve, then that does not mean you are a failure. Measure success by your own metric. What is healthy for *you*? What do <u>you</u> want to do with your life? Once you find that, stick to it. The path towards self-actualization is long, challenging, and a bit tedious at times, but the reward is worth it. The reward, of course, is the journey to it. Learn to love the process of self-improvement.

Conclusion

Once again, I would like to thank you for purchasing this book and would like to thank you even more for making it all the way to the end. While not completely comprehensive in its scope, hopefully, this book will provide you with useful tools to stop overthinking, improve yourself, and create successful habits. I recommend bookmarking or highlighting areas of this book that you would like to come back to remind yourself of the techniques and information. Some areas of this book are complicated, and there is enough information that it is difficult to commit all of it to memory in one go.

Please do not hesitate to do more research on the subject, either on your own or using some of the resources provided throughout the chapters. The literature on all of these topics is vast and deep, with many of the primary sources involving research studies and other scientific methodology in order to validate the conclusions. They're not exactly leisurely reads, but they provide a dense and detailed understanding of the topics at hand, more so than this book is intended to convey. Lastly, remember that as with anything, you need to practice.

Reading gives you the information, but practice makes it work. The next step in your journey is to act with purpose.

Finally, if you found this book useful in any way, a review on Amazon is always appreciated!

I hope you enjoyed reading, and wish you luck in all of your future endeavors.

Description

This book is about overthinking. It's also about some other things; stress, anxiety, your mind, and your emotions, to name a few. In reading this book, you should learn a couple of things.

- You'll learn what overthinking is and some of the root causes of it.
- You'll learn how your brain processes information and how it makes a lot of decisions without "thinking."
- You'll learn how to avoid procrastination and how to plan for success.
- You'll learn how to reduce anxiety through meditation and other therapeutic techniques.
- You'll be part of an ongoing discussion about the nature of the self, your place in the world, and your opportunities for reinvention.
- We'll bring all of these topics together to understand the flow state and peak human experiences.

The goal of this book is to educate the reader on these topics mentioned above, but more importantly, it aims to educate the reader and to get them thinking about themselves. This book is not a comprehensive or definitive guide to these topics. It draws from various other resources, including primary sources and research studies in psychology, biology, and philosophy. Once you've finished reading this book, it is highly recommended that you continue to think about and research any of the things you would like to learn more about. The literature on these topics is endless, and the chapters that you read only scratch the surface of the depth, nuance, and history of that literature.

Additionally, this book acts as a sort of guide to certain healthy behaviors. It talks about how to build confidence, how to cultivate healthy habits, and how to reduce stress and anxiety. If you are someone who is very anxious and/or severely struggles with mental health, a book is no replacement for talking with a certified health care professional, whether it be a doctor, a therapist, or a counselor. These people are able to provide you with individualized, personal treatment to help you become healthier. Unfortunately, due to the sort of medium that books are, it can not always offer the same personalized tips and practices. It can only offer general advice that works for most people. It might not work for every single person in the world, and that's ok. There are other resources out there that can help. If the tips in the book do not help, do some more research. There are other ways of preventing overthinking and reducing anxiety than are listed in this book.

Printed by Libri Plureos GmbH in Hamburg,
Germany